BESIDE
THE
SEASIDE

ABOUT THE AUTHOR

Jane Struthers is the author of over twenty books, including *Red Sky at Night: The Book of Lost Countryside Wisdom*, *Literary Wisdom*, *Literary Britain and Ireland* and *Britain's Coastlines from the Air*. She lives near Rye in East Sussex with her husband and two cats.

Praise for *Beside the Seaside: A Celebration of the Place We Like to Be*:

'Nautical but nice' *Daily Mail*

'An end-of-pier lucky dip of seaside fun' *Telegraph*

'Packed with enjoyable, lively and interesting anecdotes'
BBC Country File magazine

'The perfect holiday read' *Country Homes & Interiors*

BESIDE
THE
SEASIDE

A CELEBRATION OF THE
PLACE WE LIKE TO BE

Jane Struthers

EBURY
PRESS

3 5 7 9 10 8 6 4 2

First published in 2011 by Ebury Press, an imprint of Ebury Publishing
A Random House Group company

This edition published by Ebury Press in 2018

The Random House Group Limited Reg. No. 954009

Addresses for companies within the Random House Group can be found at
www.randomhouse.co.uk

A CIP catalogue record for this book is available from the British Library

The Random House Group Limited supports The Forest Stewardship
Council (FSC), the leading international forest certification organisation.
All our titles that are printed on Greenpeace approved FSC certified paper
carry the FSC logo. Our paper procurement policy can be found at
www.rbooks.co.uk/environment

Mixed Sources
Product group from well-managed
forests and other controlled sources
www.fsc.org Cert no. TT-COC-2139
© 1996 Forest Stewardship Council
FSC

Printed and bound in Great Britain by Clays Ltd, Elcograf S.p.A

ISBN 9781529102444

To buy books by your favourite authors and register for offers visit
www.rbooks.co.uk

In memory of my mother, Jean Struthers, who loved the sea and died five days after I got the go-ahead for this book – it was the last piece of news I was able to give her

CONTENTS

Foreword 11

WISH YOU WERE HERE

The rise of the seaside resort 15
Bank holiday madness 16
Hi-de-hi! 18
Piers of the realm 20
Listen to the band 22
Seaside sauce 23
All in the best possible taste 24
A nice change 27
That's the way to do it! 29

COME ON IN, THE WATER'S LOVELY!

The Moon and the tides 33
Why is the sea salty? 34
Sandy shores 36
The shingle tingle 37
Watch the flags 38
Net gain 39
A quick dip 41
Buzzing about 43
A fishy list 45

BEACH GAMES

Donkey rides 57
Ducks and drakes 58
French cricket 59
Beach volleyball 60
Digging yourselves in 61
Castles in the sand 62
Sand sculptures 64

GETTING UP AN APPETITE

A stick of rock. 67
A perfect seaside picnic 68
Fish and chips. 70
Killing with kindness. 72
Cornish heavy cake. 73
Potted shrimps 74
The knickerbocker in all its glory 75
Flapjacks. 76
The real zing. 77
To make a nice whet before dinner 78
Getting in a laver 78
Sea greens. 79
Some scrumptious shellfish 80

COASTAL LIFE

Searching for shells. 87
Salty tastes 91
The butterflies flutter by. 94
A word in your shell-like. 95
In a crabby mood 96
Clinging on like a limpet 99
Beachcombing 100
Stings and things 102
Seaward for seaweed 104
Stowaways and stranded plants 107

ALONG THE COAST

Common coastal birds 111
Seaside strolls. 114
Beachside reading 116
The Cinque Ports. 119
Taken by the sea. 120
Dangerous waters. 122
Beacons in the dark 125
Coastal curiosities 130

THE HIGH SEAS

Crossing the English Channel 135
British waters 137
Watery names. 140
Great ships. 142
John Harrison and the question of longitude. 146
The Merchant Navy 149
Who was the real Robinson Crusoe? 150

UNWELCOME VISITORS

Rule Britannia! 155
They came from the north 156
Parlez-vous français? 158
The Barbary pirates 160
'God's wind blew, and they were scattered' 162
Martello towers 164
Occupation. 165

FIFTEEN MEN ON THE DEAD MAN'S CHEST

Pirates! 171
The Jolly Roger. 172
Big bad Blackbeard 173
Pieces of eight 175
Customs and contraband. 176
A smuggler's song. 178
Wreckers! 180
On a hiding to something. 181
Desperadoes. 183
Moonrakers and owlers 185

THE SENIOR SERVICE

You're in the Navy now 191
The pride of the line. 193
First rate! 197
Sea salt 198
Time for the toast. 201
Join the Wrens and free a man for the fleet 202

FOR THOSE IN PERIL ON THE SEA

Heart of oak. 207
Press gangs. 208

Hard tack and weevils 210
The scourge of scurvy 211

KNOWING THE ROPES
Salty speech 217
At the rate of knots 219
When eight bells toll 220
The ship's bell 221
Port and starboard 222
And now the Shipping Forecast 226
Who, what and where? 228
Get knotted! 237
Take that! 238

TRADITIONS
There she blows 243
The ship's cat 244
Sea shanties 246
Guernsies, ganseys and Arans 247
I name this ship 250
A ship's figurehead 252
Down the hatch! 253

LEGENDS
Where giants walked? 259
The mysteries of St Michael's Mount 260
Of mermaids and mermen 261
The creatures of Orkney 264
Lost lands 266

SUPERSTITIONS
Setting sail 273
The dreaded albatross 274
Whistling up a storm 275
Ghost ships 276
Down in Davy Jones' locker 278

Acknowledgements 280
Index 281

FOREWORD

This precious stone set in a silver sea,
Which serves it in the office of a wall,
Or as a moat defensive to a house,
Against the envy of less happier lands;
This blessed plot, this earth, this realm, this England.

RICHARD II, WILLIAM SHAKESPEARE

Shakespeare wrote those words over 400 years ago, but for many people they still sum up the image of the British Isles as being set apart from the rest of the world. The people who live on these islands have been seafarers, with all that this entails, since they first arrived here. The sea is in the average Briton's blood, whether or not they are aware of it. It has given the country a rich and varied heritage, in more ways than we might imagine.

The British language is peppered with words that are a linguistic legacy of the long list of invaders who have landed on these shores over the centuries. Some of them, such as the Romans and Vikings, left again. Others, such as the Normans, stayed. Words and phrases that were originally used onboard ship have entered the language, and the maritime connections of some of them are almost forgotten now.

The waters around Britain have affected our lives in many other ways. The sea continues to erode some parts of the coastline and create new land elsewhere. For centuries, fishermen have risked their lives in the seas to bring home their catch. Young boys joined the Navy and sailed away. Some sailed home again, richer or poorer for the experience. Pirates struck fear in people's hearts, privateers brought back legally sanctioned plunder, smugglers helped the local economy or stole from the Crown, depending on which side of the law you stood on.

And then there is the pleasure of the seaside, of going to the beach on a hot day and feeling the scrunch of the sand between your toes, the shock of the first cold splash of seawater against your legs, the truly breathtaking experience of submerging yourself in the sparkling sea. Why is it never as warm as you'd imagined? The picnics, the beachcombing, the jaunt to the pier, the boat trip round the lighthouse, the treats of the ice-cream parlour, the struggles to get dressed and undressed without embarrassing yourself, the marvel of sand that gets everywhere.

The seaside offers different charms in the winter, when the grey sea merges into the leaden sky, you hear the repeated boom as the waves pound against the breakwaters, the spume and spray smash on to the prom in a storm, when you try to speak but your words are snatched away by the wind as the seagulls shriek and circle above you, with your hair whipped into your eyes and the tang of salt on your lips. Days when you're thankful to be on dry land and you fear for the fate of those out on the pitching seas, with Davy Jones' locker waiting for them at the bottom of the vasty deep.

These are some of the topics that you will find in this book. Tales of pirates and smugglers, of sea captains and great voyages, of superstitions and fears, of mermaids and drowned villages, of the birth of the Navy and ships of the line. Facts about sand, geology, the tides, and suggestions about how to enjoy yourself when you get to the beach. Which I hope you will, as this book reminds you of the many pleasures to be found at the seaside.

Jane Struthers
February 2011
East Sussex

WISH YOU WERE HERE

Skegness is SO bracing.

POSTER ISSUED BY THE GREAT NORTHERN RAILWAY, 1908

The Rise of the Seaside Resort

Before the middle of the 18th century, no middle-class person would ever have dreamt of setting foot on the beach. It was the preserve of working people, such as fishermen, sailors and smugglers, and no fashionable soul would have wanted to associate themselves with it.

But that was before Dr Richard Russell wrote a treatise in the early 1750s on the benefits of seawater in treating glandular diseases. Until then, people had flocked to inland spas such as those in Bath and Malvern in order to improve their health by bathing in the water and drinking it. Dr Russell proposed visiting the seaside, and especially the fishing village of Brighthelmstone (which also went by the name of Brighton), which was near to his home in Lewes, in what is now East Sussex. Perhaps he was anticipating being able to treat lots of new patients, and he certainly succeeded in that because he eventually could afford to build a large house in Brighthelmstone.

After Russell's death, his house was rented out to seasonal visitors who had come to take the waters. One of these was Prince Henry, Duke of Cumberland and Strathearn. This was already a fillip to the area, but things got even better when his brother, none other than

King George III, visited in 1779. Brighthelmstone was by now highly fashionable, so much so that it was styled the 'Paris of its day' by the *Morning Herald*. The arrival of royalty helped tremendously, and when the then Prince of Wales bought a small property called Brighton Farmhouse, Brighthelmstone's success was assured.

In due course, several important changes took place. Brighthelmstone expanded and became Brighton; the Prince of Wales became the Prince Regent and later George IV, and his Brighton Farmhouse eventually evolved into the Royal Pavilion. Another important event was the start of the Napoleonic Wars, which began in 1803. Wealthy and fashionable Britons were accustomed to going abroad for their holidays, but war with the French meant that Europe was out of bounds, so they began to visit the British seaside instead.

The development of the railway system in the mid-19th century made the seaside a more egalitarian place because so many more people were able to visit it. Better roads helped, too. Soon, holidaymakers were flocking to the seaside, and in Northern England such towns as Scarborough, Blackpool, Morecambe and Skegness began to thrive. Llandudno was known as 'The Queen of the Welsh Resorts', and many holiday resorts sprang up around the Firth of Clyde in Scotland.

It was the start of a British love affair with the seaside that has waxed and waned ever since but is unlikely to ever be eclipsed. Our bucket and spade holidays are here to stay.

Bank Holiday Madness

Lots of events helped to contribute to the popularity of a trip to the seaside, including the arrival of the steam train. But what made a huge difference to many people was an Act of Parliament in 1871. This was the Bank Holidays Act, developed by the Liberal politician Sir John Lubbock. He was a banker as well as an MP, and a big fan of cricket. The story goes that he wanted bankers to be able to attend

their village cricket matches rather than be slogging away behind a desk, so he introduced four statutory holidays a year when banks were closed and employees could don their cricket whites. These four days were Easter Monday, Whit Monday, the first Monday in August and Boxing Day. Banks already closed their doors on the two great Christian festivals of Easter Sunday and Christmas Day. Although this might seem like progress, in fact bankers had enjoyed many more holidays earlier in the century but the Industrial Revolution, with its emphasis on hard work, had put paid to those.

Bank workers weren't the only ones to benefit from the newly introduced bank holidays. Until then, Sunday was the only time shops and factories were closed so the introduction of this new holiday meant a rare extra day off for blue-collar workers. Seaside resorts soon became packed when the first Monday in August came round. Railway companies laid on extra trains, and there were extra steamers too to transport people around the coast. Everyone was determined to have a good time.

Well, perhaps not quite everyone. Some resorts refused to welcome the massive influx of holidaymakers who were often notorious for their bad behaviour. Bournemouth, which prided itself on its genteel image, got its railway in 1870 but swiftly banned all trains on Sundays in the hope that this would keep out the riff-raff – a policy that continued until 1914. Sunday steamers weren't allowed to dock there either, until Bournemouth relented in 1920.

It was all very well for thousands of people to have a holiday at the seaside over the August Bank Holiday, but where were they going to stay? There weren't enough beds for them all, which could lead to problems with public order. Sometimes holidaymakers who failed to find digs had to sleep in the open air, assuming that they could find a big enough patch of it. On August Bank Holiday in 1926, Southend's prom was turned into an informal dormitory when 10,000 people slept there. They stretched for six miles. Brighton faced the same sort of problem in the 1950s, and solved it by leaving out 2,000 deckchairs for people who couldn't find anywhere else to sleep.

Bank holidays in the early 1960s were notorious for more reasons than just a shortage of beds. It was the era of the Mods and Rockers, who regularly clashed at seaside resorts. The Mods rode scooters, wore sharply cut Italian suits and prided themselves on their very neat and ultra-fashionable appearance. The hearts of the Rockers belonged to the 1950s, not only in musical terms but also where their clothes were concerned. They rode big motorbikes, slicked back their hair and wore scruffy jeans and big leather jackets. Most of all, they hated the Mods and the Mods hated them. Huge brawls became commonplace at such seaside resorts as Brighton, Clacton, Margate and even poor old Bournemouth; the Mods and Rockers might not agree on anything else, but they certainly shared the same taste in holiday destinations.

HI-DE-HI!

'Where do you think you are? A holiday camp?' This rather sarcastic question is usually asked of people when they're thought to be slacking. But the original holiday camp was a far cry from the luxurious holiday destination it has turned into.

Although his is no longer a household name, we have Joseph Cunningham to thank for the development of holiday camps. He combined being a flour merchant with his work as a Sunday school superintendent. He also began something that became an institution for millions of people each year.

It all started with the annual summer camps that Cunningham organised for boys' institutes in Liverpool in Victorian times. These did so well that in 1894 he and his wife Elizabeth branched out and set up a holiday camp in Douglas on the Isle of Man. The criteria was strict: only teetotal young men need apply. These men also had to be content to sleep in bell tents in the open air. Despite these apparent privations, the Cunningham Camp, as it was known, was such a hit that by 1908 it had softened up a little and provided all sorts of amusements, including a vast dining room, a concert hall and a heated swimming pool. The emphasis was on good clean fun, with organised games and entertainments.

After the First World War the camp ditched the bell tents for bungalows and dormitories. Later, it rather daringly allowed girls to attend its dances, although their board and lodgings were a safe and respectable distance from the camp. It was still going strong at the start of the Second World War, when it was requisitioned for official use.

The Cunningham Camp wasn't the only holiday camp to thrive in the Edwardian era. In 1906 the Socialist Camp opened in Caister, Norfolk. As its name suggests it was founded on Socialist principles and everyone did their share of the work. The name of the camp was soon changed to the more jolly-sounding Caister Holiday Camp, which attracted middle-class holidaymakers. Once again, the original bell tents were discarded, this time being replaced by chalets. The enterprise was such a good idea that various interested parties, including trade unions, founded their own holiday camps in the years that followed.

Holiday camps really took off in the 1930s. One of the most successful brands was created by Billy Butlin, a South African who used the proceeds from his chain of amusement parks to set up holiday camps designed to appeal to what he called 'middle-income families'. He began in Skegness in 1936, with 600 chalets that enticingly offered electricity plus hot and cold running water (facilities that today we take for granted), as well as three meals a day and free entertainment. Luxury! The camp was such a hit that it doubled in capacity the following year, and eventually catered for 10,000 holidaymakers a week. A second camp opened in Clacton in 1938. Then the Second World War arrived, which put a bit of a dampener on the holiday trade. But Billy Butlin switched to building military camps that he cleverly bought back once peace had returned in 1945. He had most definitely made the most of the market: by the late 1940s, one in 20 Britons spent their holidays in a Butlins camp. And the number would have been higher if the camps had been bigger, but they were already filled to bursting.

The popularity of foreign holidays in the 1960s, followed by increasingly cheap airfare, dented the holiday camps' collective fortune, but some of them are still going strong, with their emphasis on fun for all the family.

PIERS OF THE REALM

In Victorian times, all the best seaside resorts had a pleasure pier. This was a beautiful feat of engineering skill, often with a lacy network of iron girders supporting it in the sea, and it extended from the promenade far out into the briny. Holidaymakers could stroll along it to take the air and enjoy the unusual experience of being able to view their holiday resort from a completely new angle. They might even be able to wave to their more timid friends ashore.

At first, the seaside pier was purely an opportunity to take a leisurely stroll, but when paddle steamers became popular each pier sprouted landing stages where passengers could embark and disembark.

Britain's first pier was built at Ryde, on the Isle of Wight, and was opened to the public on 26 July 1814. It began life as a wooden jetty for boats, but was extended several times during the next 40 years. It is still standing, unlike the Leith Chain Pier which was built in 1821 and the Brighton Chair Pier which was constructed two years later.

The first iron piers weren't built until the mid-19th century. Southport Pier was one of the earliest, and was opened on 2 August 1860. It's a very long pier, but it isn't the longest. That accolade goes to Southend Pier, which is so lengthy that it has its own train line to save holidaymakers the bother of walking from one end of it to the other. It replaced an older structure, and was opened on 24 August 1890. It was later extended, and in 1897 became the world's longest pier. It was even given an upper deck. The pier was requisitioned by the Admiralty during the Second World War to serve as a convoy assembly point and became known as HMS *Leigh*.

Some resorts were so popular – and wealthy – that one pier wasn't enough. Brighton, for instance, had the West Pier and the Palace Pier, until the West Pier was damaged in a storm in December 2002 and then suffered two arson attacks a few weeks later. Blackpool has not one, not two, but three piers – the Central Pier where people could dance, the North Pier which was considered much more genteel, and the South Pier, an ice-cream cornet's throw from the world-famous pleasure beach.

By their very nature, piers are vulnerable structures and many Victorian gems have fallen foul of storms, fire and old age. Roughly 100 piers graced British seaside resorts at the start of the 20th century, but now that number has almost been halved. The National Piers Society is doing its best to protect those that are left, but tight local authority budgets and arsonists may mean that the surviving piers will go out with a splash, as they gradually disappear into the sea that surrounds them.

LISTEN TO THE BAND

Oh, I do like to be beside the seaside,
Oh, I do like to be beside the sea.
Oh, I do like to stroll along the prom, prom, prom
While the brass band plays, tiddlely om pom pom.

'I DO LIKE TO BE BESIDE THE SEASIDE',
JOHN H GLOVER-KIND

And where does the brass band play? At the bandstand, of course. These sprang up in Victorian times like iron-clad mushrooms, to chime in not only with the increasing popularity of seaside holidays but also with the rise of brass bands.

Of course, bandstands appeared in parks as well, which is why many inland towns have them. They were usually either circular or semicircular, with roofs to shelter the bandsmen, open sides and plenty of space around them for everyone to listen to the music.

Some bandstands were much more decorative than others, but every seaside resort worth its salt had to have one. Some Victorian bandstands looked slightly skeletal because of their construction and design, such as the bandstand at Lytham St Anne's in Lancashire, while others like the bandstand at Westcliff-on-Sea in Essex had curved roofs that gave them the appearance of a Chinese pagoda. One of the most iconic and beautiful but more modern bandstands is in Eastbourne in East Sussex. It replaced the previous bandstand, which was built on stilts, and has an elaborate blue dome that is claimed by locals to be unique.

SEASIDE SAUCE

If you're going on a seaside holiday, one of the pleasures is sending postcards to everyone stuck at home. And the sort of card that you choose says a lot about you. As you look through the carousels of postcards outside the kiosks along the prom, you have plenty of designs to choose from. Should you choose a winsome card with a cat or a bunny on it? Or a photo of your hotel, so you can mark the location of your room with an X? Or perhaps you'd prefer to opt for another sort of seaside holiday tradition and choose a postcard with a saucy message. If so, you will be honouring the work of Donald McGill, whose naughty postcards have adorned countless mantelpieces for decades.

Although Donald McGill's postcard designs were of the nudge-nudge-wink-wink variety that relied on double entendres, eager honeymoon couples, bewildered vicars, over-endowed women and sex-starved men, he was a respectable Victorian graphic artist who said at the end of his life, 'I'm not proud of myself, I always wanted to do something better'. Although it's thought that as many as 200 million of his postcards were sold between 1904 and his death in 1962, he was paid very little money for his original designs and his contracts didn't include the payment of royalties. He even got caught up in a censorship trial in 1954, when his designs were branded as obscene. Each seaside town had its own censorship committee, which kept a beady eye on anything that it considered to be vulgar, in poor taste or downright disgusting. And one committee pounced on Donald McGill's work, which was thought to lower the tone in many of the more straitlaced seaside resorts.

McGill was found guilty under the 1857 Obscene Publications Act and fined. This did nothing for his already meagre bank balance and it also dealt a body blow to the saucy postcard industry, which never really recovered. But perhaps he had the last laugh because today his work is highly valued, not only for its light-hearted and very British humour but also for its collectability. The original artwork for what were once considered to be throwaway jokes is now very valuable. You could buy an awful lot of ice creams with that kind of money.

ALL IN THE BEST POSSIBLE TASTE

If any of the people who first used bathing machines in Britain could see what 21st-century holidaymakers wear on the beach, they would probably faint dead away and have to be revived with something a lot stronger than smelling salts. We associate the genteel practice of using bathing machines with the Victorians, but it began a long time before that.

British people first began what is now their enduring love of sea bathing in the mid-17th century. The novel idea of bathing in the sea was considered to be the latest way to improve one's health, and it was rather daring, too, which added to the excitement. And for a very good reason, because when sea bathing first began both sexes took to the water in the nude. But, as far as some resorts were concerned, this practice wasn't acceptable and modesty had to be preserved at all costs, because it would have frightened the horses and caused pandemonium if the women bathers had been seen by the men. Perhaps political correctness isn't a modern phenomenon after all.

The first bathing machines were pulled into the water by horses. The bather climbed into the machine while fully dressed, then took off their clothes in privacy and moved to the end of the machine, which featured a collapsible hood. They stood under this and were helped into the water by an attendant known as a 'dipper'. Once they were in the water, only their heads were visible. Even so, the beach was segregated into one area for men and another for women. In 1805 the bathing machines at Margate in Kent were described in W C Oulton's travellers' guide: '... the bather descending from the machine by a few steps is concealed from the public view, whereby the most refined female is enabled to enjoy the advantages of the sea with the strictest delicacy.'

Before long, men stopped swimming naked and started to wear swimming costumes. Those 'refined females' already wore long dresses, made from fabric that wouldn't turn see-through in the water (imagine the embarrassment), and with hems that were weighted down so they wouldn't float upwards. The men wore one-piece bathing suits made from wool, with long arms and legs, rather like combinations. By Victorian times, women were wearing two-piece bathing suits. But forget any ideas about bikinis. These suits consisted of a gown that covered the woman's arms and chest, and reached her knees, and a pair of bloomers that went down to her feet. After all, this was an age when the sight of a shapely female ankle was considered to be wildly shocking and provocative.

Segregated bathing continued until the late 1890s, but by then it was becoming out of date. Besides which, many people broke the rules, and mixed bathing was already all the rage in Europe and the United States. The use of bathing machines began to change, too. Bathers still changed their clothes in them, but they were happy to walk down the beach and into the sea, so the bathing machines became static and were eventually superseded by beach huts.

Bathing costumes gradually began to get smaller. The sleeves vanished, followed by the full-length bloomers, and by 1910 women had a lot more freedom in the sea. Even so, swimming costumes for both sexes were still made from flannel or wool (to keep you warm in the cold water), which often sagged most unbecomingly. By the 1920s, swimming costumes were much more streamlined, especially for women, even though they still stopped at mid-thigh for decency's sake.

By the 1940s, the development of man-made fabrics such as rayon revolutionised swimwear and it became more figure-hugging. Two-piece swimming costumes, which had first been introduced in the 1920s, became more popular for women and also a lot more daring than the original modest designs.

The bikini arrived in 1946 (named after Bikini Atoll, which had been the site of nuclear weapons tests, because it was thought that the new fashion would have a similarly explosive impact). It was very modest at first, but in the 1960s it began to look as though it had shrunk in the wash. Men continued to wear bathing shorts but these got smaller too, and those heavy wool cozzies that had drooped so unflatteringly (and sometimes dangerously) were consigned to the dustbin of history.

Today, swimwear is often tinier than ever. Thongs, monokinis, tankinis and skimpy Speedos all make regular appearances on Britain's beaches. So too, strangely enough, do long shorts for men, proving yet again that fashion goes round in circles. As do many swimmers.

A NICE CHANGE

Anyone who has ever stood on a sandy beach, wobbling about on one leg while trying to pull up their underwear over their sea-damp legs with one hand and holding the towel protecting their modesty with the other, will understand the attractions of the beach hut.

This is a small, wooden construction that is usually sited very close to the beach, so bathers don't have far to walk to get into the sea. It has a door that you can shut behind you, to keep you safe from prying eyes. There is space to hang up your clothes without having to worry about them getting full of sand, which is what can so easily happen on the beach, and some beach huts even have electricity or bottled gas so you can boil a kettle for a nice cup of tea. On days when the sun is out but the wind is up, you can shelter in your beach hut, which is so much more elegant than battling with a striped canvas windbreak that will probably be blown on top of you as soon as you finally lower yourself into your deckchair.

Beach huts were a mid-Victorian invention, and were the obvious successor to bathing machines. At first, they were converted bathing machines or fishermen's huts, but as their popularity grew many seaside promenades sported neat lines of purpose-built, modern constructions. Bournemouth in Dorset was one of the first towns to have these, built on the prom on either side of the pier in about 1909.

As with just about everything in Britain, class distinctions prevailed and in the early 20th century beach huts were considered to be the province of 'the toiling classes', as they were called. Few self-respecting middle-class people who weren't toiling would want to associate themselves with such things, but beach huts became much more appealing after 1929, when George V and Queen Mary spent 13 weeks at Bognor in Sussex while the king recovered from a lung operation. Suddenly, everything connected with the seaside had become ultra-smart, and that included beach huts. Some were privately owned and others could be rented from the local council.

All British beaches were off-limits during the Second World War and the beach huts were locked up for the duration, but they were back to their sandy selves after the war was over and really came into their own as everyone flocked back to the seaside with their buckets and spades.

Today, some beach huts can still be rented from local councils but many more are in private hands. If you are lucky enough to find one that's for sale, it will cost a lot more than you might imagine, especially if the council has granted the right to stay in it overnight. It depends, of course, on the part of the British coastline that you've got your eye on, but even the cheapest hut will cost several thousand pounds.

If such seaside splendours are beyond your means but you are very concerned about decorously changing your clothes on the beach, you might consider a much more modest proposal. It doesn't have the cachet of a hut smartly painted in blue and white stripes, but it is certainly a throwback to the 1960s when beaches were covered in such things. Think of it as your own portable beach hut. One that you can shelter under when the wind hurls sand at you and which will enable you to pull off your wet swimming togs and put on your dry clothes without giving the rest of the beach a cheap thrill. And you can create it at home in almost no time at all. All you need are two huge bath towels (preferably in a jaunty pattern) or one long piece of towelling which you cut in half. Sew the long ends together to make a tube. Make a hem at one end of the tube and thread a thick piece of elastic through it until it's big enough to go over your head and sit on your shoulders. If necessary, hem the other end to stop it fraying. Voila! Your very own beach tent.

And next time you are taking your clothes off under it in comfort you might realise that it makes a very nice change indeed.

THAT'S THE WAY TO DO IT!

In these days of political correctness it might be difficult to believe that part of a traditional British seaside holiday involves children avidly watching a puppet show featuring a hunchbacked, violent husband, his equally violent wife, their hapless baby, a policeman and a dog called Toby. But that's what you get if you watch a Punch and Judy show. And long may it last.

The traditional show is performed by a single puppeteer (often called 'the Professor'), who is hidden from view in a striped kiosk. Punch, Judy and the rest of the cast are glove puppets, and because they are operated by one person only two puppets can appear on the stage at the same time. However, that restriction is more than compensated for with a large cast of characters, not only human but animal and also spectral.

Today, Punch and Judy shows are fairly modest affairs, but back in the 17th century, when they first appeared in Britain, they were much more lavish and were performed with marionettes (puppets operated with strings). It's believed that Mr Punch, as he became known, made his debut in the British theatre on 9 May 1662, when Samuel Pepys noted in his diary that he saw 'an Italian puppet play' at Covent Garden. It was, he said, 'the best that ever I saw'. It was performed by Signor Pietro Gimonde (popularly known as Signor Bologna) and featured a character called Pulchinello, who came from the Italian commedia dell'arte. Pepys took his wife to the show a couple of weeks later, and Charles II was in the audience later that year.

At first, the hook-nosed, hunchbacked, shrill-voiced puppet was called Pulchinello, just as in his native Italy, and his wife was called Joan, but eventually he became known as Mr Punch and her name was changed to Judy. In the following years, Punch and Judy flourished as marionette shows, but by the end of the 18th century they cost so much to produce that they were superseded by glove puppets.

As seaside holidays became more popular in late Victorian times, thanks to the introduction of the bank holiday, Punch and Judy shows began to appear in the new holiday resorts.

The plot of a typical show is fluid and easy to follow. It always involves Punch being asked by his wife to carry out some simple instructions, such as taking care of their baby, his inability to do so and the dreadful consequences that always involve much bashing of one another with sticks. Cue the policeman, a snapping-jawed crocodile, and even Jack Ketch the hangman. But no matter what terrible fate awaits Punch, he always manages to get the better of everyone. And as he does so, he always shrieks, 'That's the way to do it!'

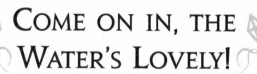

COME ON IN, THE WATER'S LOVELY!

In spite of all their friends could say,
On a winter's morn, on a stormy day
In a sieve they went to sea.

'THE JUMBLIES', EDWARD LEAR

The Moon and the Tides

I f you have ever rushed down to the seaside on a boiling hot day, ready to spread your towel on the sand and then wander down to the sea's edge, you will know how frustrating it can be to discover that you've arrived at high tide and there is hardly a scrap of beach left to sit on.

✺ Time and tide ✺

Most of the tides around the British Isles sweep into shore and out again on average every 12 hours and 25 minutes, which means that high tide follows 6 hours and just over 12 minutes after low tide. These twice-daily tides are known as semidiurnal tides. However, some parts of Britain have a different form of tide, as a result of the geography of the coastline and the depth of the sea. For instance, Portland in Devon has double-low water, because the tide comes in, goes out again slightly and then comes in again before going out as far as it is able. Just down the coast in Southampton, Hampshire, there is a double-high water. Some British coastal regions have very pronounced low and high tides, while others have less extreme tides. In other parts of the world, there are places that only have one tide a day. This is called a diurnal tide.

But what causes the tides and the subsequent variations in sea level? It is the relationship between the Earth, the Moon and the Sun, so the daily rhythm of the tides is a good reminder that we live on a planet and that it's part of the solar system. The Moon's gravitational pull on the Earth's surface is just over twice as strong as that of the Sun, which means that the water in the Earth's oceans bulges at two points: the point directly towards the Moon and the opposing point on the other side of the world. The high and low tides each day are caused by the Earth rotating on its axis beneath these bulges. They are known as lunar tides.

～ Spring and neap tides ～

The Sun also influences the tides, when they are called solar tides. Every two weeks, these have an impact on the lunar tides, either by making them more powerful or less powerful. Spring tides – which have absolutely nothing to do with the season and occur all year round – happen when the Sun and Moon are either conjunct at a New Moon or in opposition at a Full Moon. The gravitational pull of the Sun and Moon is reinforced, producing tides at their maximum range. This means the low tide is lower than normal and the high tide is higher.

A neap tide occurs at the time of the Quarter Moon – the time when the Moon is 90° away from the Sun. The tide-producing effects of the Sun and Moon cancel one another out, so the tidal ranges are at their least extreme.

New Moon	Sun conjunct Moon	Spring tide	0 days
1st Quarter Moon	Sun square Moon	Neap tide	7 days
Full Moon	Sun opposition Moon	Spring tide	14 days
2nd Quarter Moon	Sun square Moon	Neap tide	21 days

WHY IS THE SEA SALTY?

If you have ever swallowed a mouthful of seawater you'll know how salty it is. But as you pull a face and take the taste away with something sweet, have you ever wondered why the sea is salty?

There are several reasons, and they all combine to create the current level of about 3.5 per cent salinity in the world's seas. First, you have to consider where seawater comes from. The vast majority of it is transported to each of the world's seas from the rivers that flow into them. As the rivers flow through the land they collect mineral deposits from the rocks and earth, and they also wash salt out of the rocks. All this continually flows into the sea, where it stays.

Water also falls into the sea whenever it rains. Although rainwater is often described as being pure it picks up many minerals and some pollution too as it falls through the atmosphere, and this is deposited in the sea as well.

But that's not the end of the story. The salt in the sea is mostly sodium chloride. When the oceans were formed, the process generated the sodium, which is now caught in layers of sediment on the ocean beds. The chloride constituent of salt is continuously provided by the hydrothermal vents. These vents are areas on the ocean floor where seawater seeps into the oceanic crust. The water gradually becomes hotter until it dissolves some of the minerals in the rock, which seep out into the seawater. Submarine volcanoes also introduce chloride into seawater by heating the rocks until they become molten and release some of their minerals.

Scientists believe that the level of salinity in the oceans has been stable for millions, if not billions, of years. Why? You might imagine that the amount of salt would become greater as time goes on, because surely it would accumulate in the seas. After all, even though the seawater can evaporate, the salt is left behind. Its level can't only be controlled by swimmers swallowing it as they thrash about in the water. The theory is that some of the salt is trapped within the Earth's crust as the vast continental plates gradually slide over one another. Also, the sea salt creates a chemical reaction with underwater rocks, volcanic deposits and the rocks of the ocean's crust, and by doing so actually removes some of the dissolved salts from the oceans. All of this is a continual process, so the sea's salinity is always kept at its current level.

SANDY SHORES

When you're sitting on the beach, gazing out to sea or wondering whether you can sneak the last bit of cake while no one is looking and then pretend it was stolen by a seagull, the sand around you looks a uniform colour. Unless you're on a white sand beach or one filled with black volcanic sand, your particular type of sand will probably be a muddy yellow colour. And you might think that's how it is when viewed close up. But if you were to examine a handful of sand under a microscope you would realise that it's made up of many different coloured grains. So many, in fact, that it can look like something from a pick 'n' mix sweet stand.

The main ingredient is probably silica, in the form of quartz. This is a very hard rock and is most resistant to weathering – the term given to the gradual erosion of rocks by wind, rain, heat, frost and other actions of the weather. The sand can contain many other pieces of rock as well, including tiny specks of seashells.

This is the clue to how sand is created. It was once large rocks or intact shells, which have been continually bashed together by the action of the waves as they repeatedly crash against the shoreline and rocky coasts. So what was once a huge boulder gradually becomes smaller chunks of rock, then pebbles, and then shingle, and then sand. And the sand is gradually being worn away as well, until the individual grains become so tiny that they turn into minute particles of silt.

Some beaches in the United Kingdom are renowned for their especially beautiful sand. The sands of Alum Bay on the Isle of Wight are multicoloured, thanks to oxidised iron compounds that have been formed under various conditions to give the cliffs their characteristic colours. In all, there are 21 different shades of sand at Alum Bay, and the traditional gift to bring home from the Isle of Wight is a glass object filled with different layers of the sand. Holidaymakers have been doing it since Victorian times.

THE SHINGLE TINGLE

Shingle beaches are continually on the move. Whenever the tide comes in it disturbs the layers of shingle, not only eroding them by a minute amount but also distributing them around the beach. They get pushed up the beach as each wave comes in, and get dragged back down the beach as that wave retreats.

You are most likely to find a shingle beach in southern and eastern England, and particularly near chalk cliffs. The shingle is composed of small stones from what can be a rich variety of rocks, and their edges are gradually worn smooth by the continual action of the sea and the wind. Shingle looks particularly beautiful when it's wet, as the water highlights its wonderful colours and shapes.

It can be painful walking barefoot on large pebbles but shingle is normally more forgiving. Even so, it is extraordinary how often you will find a sharp bit digging into the soles of your feet.

Here are some of the rocks that make up the shingle on Britain's shores. Some of them, such as carnelian and jasper, will be well known to anyone who uses crystals.

Agate	greenish-yellow
Basalt	black
Carnelian	pinky-orange
Chalk	white
Citrine	yellow or orange
Flint	grey

Granite	speckled grey
Jasper	red
Jet	black and shiny
Limestone	pale grey
Quartz	opalescent white
Red sandstone	deep pink
Serpentine	turquoise
Shale	matt grey

WATCH THE FLAGS

Walking or playing on the beach or swimming in the sea are some of life's greatest pleasures but you must make sure you're safe and you must always act responsibly. The weather conditions are an obvious indicator – most people don't want to go near the sea during a storm. At the very least, you're likely to be drenched in sea spray. At the worst, you could be swept away by the waves and drowned, and the lives of coastguards or lifeboat crew will be endangered when they try to find you.

Another way of knowing whether it's safe to be on the beach or in the water is to look at the flags that will be flying nearby. There are four different flags, each of which carries its own specific message.

RED AND YELLOW FLAG This indicates an area where lifeguards operate. This means it's the safest place to paddle, swim or to use an inflatable.

BLACK AND WHITE CHEQUERED FLAG This area is not safe for swimmers or bodyboarders, who must avoid it. It's an area of the beach and sea devoted to surfboards, kayaks and similar craft.

ORANGE WINDSOCK This either indicates offshore winds (winds blowing from the land towards the sea) which might carry you out to sea, or it warns that the water conditions are unsafe. Inflatables should never be used when an orange windsock is flying.

RED FLAG This is a danger sign, showing that no one should enter the sea, regardless of the circumstances.

NET GAIN

S ome things never change. Fishermen have used nets to catch their fish for millennia. It's the best way to sweep up a big catch, and each type of net is used for a specific purpose. These are some of the nets that are used around Britain's coastlines.

FYKE NET To landlubbers, this looks like a most peculiar net – rather like a fishnet stocking containing a series of stainless steel rings. Fyke nets with large mesh are used to catch large fish because they can't see the mesh very well. Nets with a finer mesh can be used for smaller fish. A series of fyke nets can be held together with chains when it isn't possible to use larger traps.

GILL NET This is rather like a tennis net – it is long and narrow, and it's stretched out on the seabed, with buoyancy floats that mark its position. The fish try to swim through it but they get stuck, and they can't swim backwards because their gills have been caught in the mesh. The fisherman removes them by hand. Different sizes of mesh are used to catch different species of fish.

LOBSTER POT These come in various sizes and shapes but they all consist of a solid frame that is covered with sturdy netting. The idea is that the lobster can crawl into the pot, lured by some fishy bait left in the 'kitchen', then crawls into another part of the pot called the 'parlour' where it can't escape. The lobster pot is left on the seabed, its position marked by a buoy that floats on the water. When the fisherman returns, with luck there are lobsters or crayfish waiting in the pot.

Crab pots have a different design but perform the same function.

PURSE SEINE NET This is a large, rectangular fishing net, particularly suited to catching fish that swim in shoals, such as mackerel, herring, sardines and anchovies. It is weighted along the bottom edge and has buoyant floats on the top edge. It is arranged in a semicircle, and a rope runs through a sequence of rings on the bottom edge. The idea is simple: the shoal of fish swims into the net, then the rope along the bottom is pulled tight and the net closes around the fish.

A QUICK DIP

On a cold winter's day, what could be better than cuddling up in front of a log fire, toasting your toes – not to mention a plateful of tea cakes – in front of its warmth? Where else would you want to be? Well, that rather depends. For a small but select section of the population, there is another option: swimming in the sea. Even if they have to shiver across an icy beach to get there.

Some people like to celebrate Christmas or the New Year by immersing themselves in the briny for a couple of heart-stopping minutes. These teeth-chattering dips often draw the photographers and news teams. But other swimmers like to get into the sea almost every day, regardless of the date on the calendar.

There's nothing new in the idea. A century ago, Britain abounded in outdoor swimming clubs, full of hardy souls who were happy to brave the elements throughout the year. They swam in rivers, lakes, estuaries and, of course, in the sea itself. Some of them wore swimming costumes but others didn't bother. However, very often those who preferred to wear their birthday suits when diving off the end of the local pier had to do so early in the morning, before the rest of the world was about, to avoid shocking any women who happened to be passing. (Any woman who was up earlier than that was generally deemed to be no better than she ought to be.) Some of those swimming clubs still thrive, kept afloat by people who prefer 'wild swimming', as it's often called, to being doused in chlorine in municipal swimming pools.

Swimming in the sea can take some getting used to, especially if you normally splash about in your local swimming baths. There are no lanes to follow, the shallow end is almost non-existent at high tide and sometimes the water is so choppy that you seem to swallow it rather than swim in it. You also have to be wary of strong currents, rocks, tidal rips, litter and other hazards. It's wise to swim with other people in case one of you gets into difficulties, and it's essential to use your common sense. Know your limits, wear a coloured bathing cap that will make it easy to see you if you get into deep water and build up your swimming time gradually. You might be able to power up and down a swimming pool with ease, but you'll find it an entirely different matter when you have to cope with the strength and force of the waves on a windy day.

There is also the matter of water temperature. Municipal swimming pools are usually heated. The sea, however, doesn't offer this luxury. Even on a hot summer's day, the water can feel surprisingly cold at first. So imagine how it might strike you on a chilly day in April, which is usually the month when Britain's sea temperatures are at their lowest. At this time of year, it makes sense to wear a wetsuit, plus a silicon cap and gloves. It also makes sense to acclimatise yourself gradually, and even then to spend only a few minutes in the water to avoid any risk of hypothermia. Although you will begin to feel warm as your circulation speeds up to compensate for the sea's low temperature, you will soon start to get cold again as your body diverts your blood from your arms and legs to your trunk in order to keep your organs warm. And when that happens your limbs may stop working properly, so you will find it harder to swim or even to stand upright in a heavy sea. Have a dry towel, warm clothes and a hot drink waiting for you on the shore.

You might wonder why anyone would ever be crazy enough to leap into the sea at the coldest time of year. But wild swimmers are convinced of the benefits. Not only does wild swimming boost your mood and give your skin an invigorating tingle that can last for the rest of the day, but it has also been medically proven to improve the circulation and strengthen the immune system.

Anyone fancy a dip?

BUZZING ABOUT

Britain's coastlines are full of activity. There's plenty to do if you get bored with swimming, with all manner of sports to choose from. Some of these sports are confined to designated beaches for safety reasons.

BODYBOARDING This is similar to surfing, except that the board (also known as a 'boogie board') is smaller and made from foam to fit the weight and height of its owner. There are various riding styles, ranging from lying on your stomach to standing upright.

KITESURFING Many people avoid the beach on cold windy days, but the conditions are exactly what kitesurfers are looking for. As its name suggests, kitesurfing involves surfing the water on a surfboard while being attached to a kite. When you know what you're doing, you can even fly while kitesurfing.

JET-SKIING A jet-ski is a one-person craft that's powered by an engine, rather like a mini motorboat. The sport often gets a bad name because jet-skis are noisy machines that can interrupt the enjoyment of an afternoon spent splashing about in the sea.

PARASAILING Also known as parascending, this involves being towed behind a motorboat while wearing a special form of parachute. As the boat picks up speed, you ascend into the air.

SURFING Once the preserve of bronzed beauties in Australia and the United States, surfing is now highly popular in Britain. Although you might think that south-west England, and particularly Newquay in Cornwall, is the best place for surfing, Scarborough in North Yorkshire is becoming increasingly popular.

WATERSKIING Not so long ago, this was the main water sport in the United Kingdom. Now, with such a plethora of new sports, it almost seems quaintly old-fashioned. The waterskier is towed behind a motorboat while wearing a pair of waterskis. There are several variations, including wakeboarding which involves being attached to a single board that's similar to a surfboard.

WINDSURFING This is a cross between sailing and surfing, because you stand on what is effectively a surfboard with a sail attached to it. It's an Olympic sport and is a lot trickier than it looks.

A FISHY LIST

The waters around the British Isles are teeming with fish. Some of them are easily recognisable but others look quite strange. Some are occasional visitors, possibly lured by the increased temperatures of the British waters. Others are much more common. And some of them are firmly on the list of endangered species.

Some of these fish regularly appear on fishmongers' slabs, while others would prefer to eat us rather than the other way round. Although some of these fish can be found close to the shore, many of them live far out at sea.

Allis shad (*Alosa alosa*)

Amberjack (*Seriola dumerili*)

Anchovy (*Engraulis encrasicolus*)

Angler fish (*Lophius piscatorius*)

Argentine (*Argentina sphyraena*)

Armoured bullhead, or pogge (*Agonus cataphractus*)

Atlantic bonito (*Sarda sarda*)

Ballan wrasse (*Labrus bergylta*)

Barrelfish (*Hyperoglyphe perciformis*)

Basking shark (*Cetorhinus maximus*)

Bass (*Dicentrachus labrax*)
Bermuda chub (*Kyphosus sectator*)
Beryx (*Beryx decadactylus*)
Bib, pout whiting or pouting (*Trisopterus luscus*)
Bigeye thresher shark (*Alopias superciliosus*)
Big-scale sand smelt (*Atherina boyeri*)
Black-face blenny (*Tripterygion delaisi*)
Black-fish (*Centrolophus niger*)
Black goby (*Gobius niger*)
Blackmouth dogfish (*Galeus melastomus*)
Black sea bream (*Spondyliosoma cantharus*)
Blenny (*Lipophrys pholis*)
Bloch's topknot (*Phrynorhombus regius*)
Blonde ray (*Raja brachyura*)
Blue ling (*Molva dipterygia*)
Bluemouth (*Helicolenus dactylopterus*)
Blue shark (*Prionace glauca*)
Blue whiting (*Micromesistius poutassou*)
Blunt-nosed six-gill shark (*Hexanchus griseus*)
Boar-fish (*Capros aper*)
Bogue (*Boops boops*)
Bramble shark (*Echinorhinus brucus*)
Brill (*Scophthalmus rhombus*)
Broad-nosed pipefish (*Syngnathus typhle*)

Butterfish (*Pholis gunnellus*)
Butterfly blenny (*Blennius ocellaris*)
Catfish (*Anarhichas lupus*)
Coalfish, or saithe (*Pollachius virens*)
Chub mackerel (*Scomber japonicus*)
Cod (*Gadus morhua*)
Comber (*Serranus cabrilla*)
Common eel (*Anguilla anguilla*)
Common goby (*Pomatoschistus microps*)
Common sea bream (*Pagrus pagrus*)
Common skate (*Dipturus batis*)
Common smooth-hound (*Mustelus mustelus*)
Conger eel (*Conger conger*)
Connemara clingfish (*Lepadogaster candollei*)
Corbin's sandeel (*Hyperoplus immaculatus*)
Corkwing wrasse (*Symphodus melops*)
Crystal goby (*Crystallogobius linearis*)
Cuckoo ray (*Raja naevus*)
Cuckoo wasse (*Labrus bimaculatus*)
Cusk eel (*Lamprogammus shcherbachevi*)
Dab (*Limanda limanda*)
Darkie Charlie (*Scymnorhinus licha*)
Deal-fish (*Trachipterus arcticus*)
Dentex (*Dentex dentex*)
Derbio (*Trachinotus ovatus*)
Diminutive goby (*Lebetus scorpioides*)
Dragonet (*Callionymus lyra*)
Drumfish, or meagre (*Argyrosomus regius*)
Dusky perch (*Epinephelus marginatus*)
Eagle ray (*Myliobatis aquila*)
Eelpout (*Zoarces viviparous*)
Electric ray (*Torpedo nobiliana*)

Four-bearded rockling (*Enchelyopus cimbrius*)
Five-bearded rockling (*Ciliata mustela*)
Flounder (*Platichthys flesus*)
Fries' goby (*Lesueurigobius friesii*)
Frigate mackerel (*Auxis rochei*)
Frilled shark (*Chlamydoselachus anguineus*)
Garfish (*Belone belone*)
Giant goby (*Gobius cobitis*)
Gilthead (*Sparus aurata*)
Golden grey mullet (*Liza aurata*)
Goldsinny (*Ctenolabrus rupestris*)
Greater Argentine (*Argentina silus*)
Greater forked-beard (*Phycis blennoides*)
Greater sandeel (*Hyperoplus lanceolatus*)
Greater spotted dogfish (*Scyliorhinus stellaris*)
Greater weever (*Trachinus draco*)
Great pipefish (*Syngnathus acus*)
Greenland halibut (*Reinharditius hippoglossoides*)
Greenland shark (*Somniosus microcephalus*)
Grey gurnard (*Eutrigla gurnardus*)
Guinean amberjack (*Seriola carpenteri*)
Haddock (*Melanogrammus aeglefinus*)
Hagfish (*Myxine glutinosa*)
Hake (*Merluccius merluccius*)
Halibut (*Hippoglossus hippoglossus*)
Hammerhead shark (*Sphyma zygaena*)
Herring (*Clupea harengus*)
Horse mackerel, or scad (*Trachurus trachurus*)
John Dory (*Zeus faber*)
Lampern (*Lampetra fluviatilis*)
Lamprey (*Petromyzon marinus*)
Lemon sole (*Microstomus kitt*)

Leopard-spotted goby (*Thorogobius ephippiatus*)
Lesser pipefish (*Syngnathus rostellatus*)
Lesser sandeel (*Ammodytes tobianus*)
Lesser spotted dogfish (*Scyliorhinus canicula*)
Lesser weever (*Echilichthys vipera*)
Ling (*Molva molva*)
Long-finned bream (*Taractichthys longipinnis*)
Long-finned gurnard (*Aspitrigla obscura*)
Long-nosed skate (*Dipturus oxyrinchus*)
Long rough dab (*Hippoglossoides platessoides*)
Long-spined bullhead (*Taurulus bubalis*)
Louvar (*Luvarus imperialis*)

Lumpsucker (*Cyclopterus lumpus*)
Mackerel (*Scomber scombrus*)
Marbled electric ray (*Torpedo marmorata*)
Meagre, or drumfish (*Argyrosomus regius*)
Megrim (*Lepidorhombus whiffiagonis*)
Monkfish (*Squatina squatina*)
Montagu's blenny (*Coryphoblennius galerita*)
Montagu's sea snail (*Liparis montagui*)
Moray eel (*Muraena helena*)
Northern rockling (*Ciliata septentrionalis*)
Norway bullhead (*Taurulus lilljeborgi*)
Norway pout (*Trisopterus esmarki*)
Norwegian topknot (*Phrynorhombus norvegicus*)

Norwegian skate (*Dipturus oxyrinchus*)
Oar-fish (*Regalecus glesne*)
Opah (*Lampris guttatus*)
Orange roughy (*Heplostethus atlanticus*)
Painted goby (*Pomatoschistus pictus*)
Pandora (*Pagellus erythrinus*)
Pilchard (*Sardina pilchardus*)
Pilot fish (*Naucrates ductor*)
Piper (*Trigla lyra*)
Plaice (*Pleuronectes platessa*)
Pogge, or armoured bullhead (*Agonus cataphractus*)
Pollack (*Pollachius pollachius*)
Poor cod (*Trisopterus minutus*)
Porbeagle shark (*Lamna nasus*)
Pouting, bib or pout whiting (*Trisopterus luscus*)
Pout whiting, bib or pouting (*Trisopterus luscus*)
Raitt's sandeel (*Ammodytes marinus*)
Ratfish (*Chimaera monstrosa*)
Ray's bream (*Brama brama*)
Red band-fish (*Cepola rubescens*)
Red blenny (*Parablennius ruber*)
Red-fish (*Sebastes marinus*)
Red gurnard (*Aspitrigla cuculus*)
Red mullet (*Mullus surmuletus*)
Red sea bream (*Pagellus bogareveo*)
Remora (*Remora remora*)

Reticulated dragonet (*Callionymus reticulatus*)
Rock cook (*Centrolabrus exoletus*)
Rock goby (*Gobius paganellus*)
Rough fish (*Heplostethus mediterraneus*)
Saddled bream (*Oblada melanura*)
Saithe, or coalfish (*Pollachius virens*)
Salmon (*Salmo salar*)
Sand goby (*Pomatoschistus minutus*)
Sand smelt (*Atherina presbyter*)
Sand sole (*Solea lascaris*)
Sandy ray (*Raja circularis*)
Saupe (*Sarpa salpa*)
Scad, or horse mackerel (*Trachurus trachurus*)
Scaldfish (*Amoglossus laterna*)
Scale-eyed wrasse (*Acantholabrus palloni*)
Seahorse, long-snouted (*Hippocampus ramulosus*)
Seahorse, short-snouted (*Hippocampus hippocampus*)
Sea snail (*Liparis liparis*)
Sea stickleback (*Spinachia spinachia*)
Sea trout (*Salmo trutta* morpha *trutta*)
Shagreen ray (*Raja fullonica*)
Sharp-back sharp (*Oxynotus paradoxus*)
Shore clingfish (*Lepadogaster lepadogaster*)
Shore rockling (*Gaidropsaurus mediterraneus*)
Short-fin mako shark (*Isurus oxyrinchus*)
Short-spined bullhead (*Myoxocephalus scorpius*)
Silver pout (*Gadiculus argenteus*)
Skipper (*Scomberesox saurus*)
Slender sunfish (*Ranzania laevis*)
Small-eyed ray (*Raja microocellata*)
Small-headed clingfish (*Apletodon dentatus*)
Smelt (*Osmerus eperlanus*)

Smooth sandeel (*Gymnammodytes semisquamatus*)

Snake blenny (*Lumpenus lampretaeformis*)

Snake pipefish (*Entelurus aequoreus*)

Snipefish (*Macroramphosus scolopax*)

Sole (*Solea solea*)

Solenette (*Buglossidium luteum*)

Spanish bream (*Pagellus acarne*)

Spined goby (*Buenia jeffreysii*)

Spotted catfish (*Anarhichas minor*)

Spotted dragonet (*Callionymus maculatus*)

Spotted ray (*Raja montagui*)

Sprat (*Sprattus sprattus*)

Spurdog (*Squalus acanthias*)

Starry ray (*Raja radiata*)

Starry smooth-hound (*Mustelus asterias*)

Straight-nosed pipefish (*Nerophis ophidion*)

Streaked gurnard (*Trigloporus lastoviza*)

Sturgeon (*Acipenser sturio*)

Sunfish (*Mola mola*)

Tadpole fish (*Raniceps raninus*)

Ten-spined stickleback (*Pungitius pungitius*)

Thick-backed sole (*Microchirus variegates*)

Thick-lipped grey mullet (*Chelon labrosus*)

Thin-lipped grey mullet (*Liza ramada*)

Thornback ray (*Raja clavata*)

Three-bearded rockling (*Gaidropsaurus vulgaris*)

Three-spined stickleback (*Gasterosteus aculcatus*)

Thresher shark (*Alopias vulpinus*)

Tompot blenny (*Parablennius gattorugine*)

Tope (*Galeorhinus galeus*)

Topknot (*Zeugopterus punctatus*)

Torsk (*Brosme brosme*)

Transparent goby (*Aphia minuta*)
Triggerfish (*Balistes capriscus*)
Tub gurnard (*Chelidonichthys lucema*)
Turbot (*Psetta maxima*)
Twaite shad (*Alosa fallax*)
Two-spot goby (*Gobiusculus flavescens*)
Two-spotted clingfish (*Diplecogaster bimaculata*)
Undulate ray (*Raja undulata*)
White sea bream (*Diplodus sargus*)
White skate (*Raja alba*)
Whiting (*Merlangius merlangus*)
Witch (*Glyptocephalus cynoglossus*)
Worm pipefish (*Nerophis lumbriciformis*)
Wreckfish (*Polyprion americanus*)
Yarrell's blenny (*Chirolophis ascanii*)

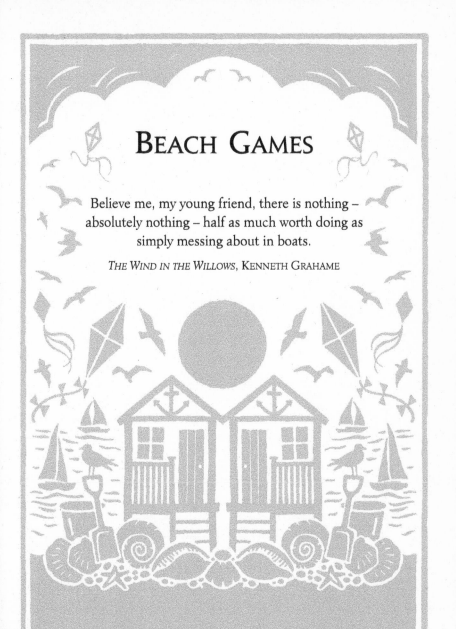

BEACH GAMES

Believe me, my young friend, there is nothing –
absolutely nothing – half as much worth doing as
simply messing about in boats.

THE WIND IN THE WILLOWS, KENNETH GRAHAME

DONKEY RIDES

You might not think that donkeys and beaches go together, but for years it was a common sight to see donkeys taking children for rides across sandy beaches. The donkeys wore colourful head-collars with their names on them, and were equipped with saddles and stirrups. Each donkey was led by an adult in the unlikely event that it would decide to cart its small passenger from one side of the beach to the other at top speed, ploughing through sandcastles as it went.

Having a ride on a beach donkey is a tradition that began in Victorian times and was popular up and down the British seaside for decades. Today, though, it has largely died out except in a few large resorts where gallant donkeys continue to help make a small child's day. The donkeys in question have to be gentle, unflustered, tolerant and quite happy to be enthusiastically patted by small, sticky hands.

Although their popularity may be dying out, the welfare of beach donkeys has probably never been higher. Each animal must be licensed and its owner must abide by a set of regulations to ensure it is properly cared for, not only during the summer but also during the winter when it is put out to pasture for a well-earned holiday.

Which is the best donkey on the British beaches? This question is settled in an annual Best Beach Donkey competition, which is organised by the Donkey Sanctuary. This is one of the main donkey charities in the country, ensuring that all the working donkeys are properly cared for and are given decent rest periods during the summer season.

DUCKS AND DRAKES

This is a beach game for days when the sea is calm and no one else is around. You can't play it when the beach is full of people, for reasons that will soon become obvious. Well, you probably could, provided that you are prepared to put in a massive burst of speed as you race down the prom followed by a lot of angry (and bruised) sea bathers. It's too antisocial a game to play on a crowded beach.

The aim of ducks and drakes is to see how many times you can skim a pebble or stone across the surface of the sea before it sinks into the briny. There is a great art to this, and it's not nearly as easy as it looks. If you're looking for hints, it helps to choose a flattened pebble and to skim it at an angle of about 20° to the surface of the water.

If you get really confident about your ability to play ducks and drakes by sending your pebble right out to sea, you could always take part in a competition. If you excel at sending your pebble far out to sea before it disappears, you can try your luck (although you may prefer to call it skill) in the annual World Championships that are held in Easdale in Scotland.

Alternatively, if bounces rather than distance are your forte, you could try your luck at beating the world record, as recorded in the *Guinness Book of Records*. But you need plenty of bounces. The world record currently stands (or skims) at 51 bounces. You can't help wondering how anyone was able to count them.

FRENCH CRICKET

Here's a good game to play when everyone needs a break from splashing about in the water or is getting a little chilly and could do with warming themselves up. It's similar to ordinary cricket but much less complicated and requires only a few players. The only equipment you need is a tennis ball (much softer than a cricket ball) and a cricket bat, tennis racquet or something else with which to whack the ball. You don't need stumps, because those are supplied by the legs of whoever is holding the bat.

The batter stands with their legs together, holding the bat or racquet in front of their legs. They often hit the ball with a scooping motion, lifting the ball into the air. The rest of the team acts as fielders. They stand around the batter in a semicircle, with the aim of dismissing him or her from the game. They can either do this by catching the ball after the batter has hit it or by hitting the stumps which are, of course, the batter's legs. This is why it's a good idea to use a ball intended for tennis rather than cricket because it doesn't hurt as much when it connects with the batter's shins. The person who caught out the batter then goes in to bat themselves.

Do the French play this form of cricket? No, they don't. It's thought that the game gets its name as a form of mockery, not only of the French but also of the sport. And you might think that really isn't cricket.

BEACH VOLLEYBALL

This is now an Olympic sport, and it goes without saying that its growing popularity has no connection with the bikini uniform of the female players and the shorts of the men. Not a jot. No, no. Perish the thought.

You can create your own volleyball game, albeit with much simpler rules, and become your own Olympic committee by choosing your own uniform. All you need is a volleyball or football, plus something to act as a net. If you don't fancy buying a real volleyball net, you could improvise with a beach windbreak or some green garden netting threaded through two bamboo sticks.

It's a good idea to slather on plenty of sunscreen before you start playing. It is also wise to avoid playing during the hottest part of the day, especially if it's already a scorcher or you aren't in the best of health.

As with all other beach games, do your best to play in an area that isn't full of people otherwise tempers will become frayed in no time at all. And unless you don't mind stubbing your toes repeatedly on rocks and stones, you should find a stretch of uninterrupted sand. Avoid patches of seaweed because they can be incredibly slippery, and it's not a lot of fun to end your day on the beach with a trip to the casualty department of the nearest hospital. Besides which, it would itch like mad if you got some stray sand trapped down your brand-new plaster cast.

As for the rules, they can be as simple or as complicated as you like. The very simplest rule is to keep the ball in the air all the time, so you bat it from your side of the net to the other with your hands. You score a point whenever you manage to make the ball hit the sand on your opponent's side of the net. Carry on playing until one side has scored ten points.

The beauty of this game is that you can all rush into the sea to cool off whenever you get too hot, and then carry on playing the next round.

DIGGING YOURSELVES IN

When it's really hot on the beach you can protect yourself from the worst of the heat by burying yourself in the sand. You can wriggle into the sand yourself or you can ask a friend to tuck you in, leaving your head free. It's surprisingly cool underneath the sand, although you will have to wash it all off in the sea before you get dressed, as sand really can get everywhere.

For safety's sake, it's essential to choose the right spot on the beach before you dig yourself in. You don't want to be too close to the waves, and you also don't want to find that you're lying in the middle of the main pathway to and from the ice-cream kiosk. Timing is important, too. Ideally, you should dig yourself in when the tide is still going out, rather than on the turn or starting to come back in, otherwise you might have to scramble for freedom more quickly than you expected.

Remember to put plenty of sunscreen on your face before you bury yourself in sand to avoid getting sunburn. It might be a good idea to wear a hat, too.

And finally, make sure you stay on speaking terms with your friends, perhaps by keeping them sweet by offering to pay for ice creams all round, in case you need help in digging yourself out.

CASTLES IN THE SAND

Believe it or not, there is an art to building sandcastles. The sand must have exactly the right texture, so it's neither too dry (the sandcastles will collapse at the first puff of wind) or too wet (they'll look like a melting ice cream). You also need the right equipment.

The most important element, of course, is the sand itself. It should be slightly damp and brown in colour so it holds together well. This means that if you're on a beach with plenty of sand, you should probably choose a patch between the middle and low water marks because if you move too high up the beach the sand may have completely dried out, especially on a hot and breezy day. Sand that's full of tiny pebbles won't hold together well.

Of course, you also need a bucket and spade. Avoid the fancy buckets with castellated bottoms because getting all the sand out of them in perfect shapes can be very tricky. Instead, choose a bucket that's plain, round and which has slightly sloping sides. As for the spade, it should be flat and broad, and preferably made from plastic to avoid anyone hurting themselves on a metal blade.

Dig up the sand and put it into the bucket until it's completely full. Now put in a little more. Give the sand several good whacks with the back of the spade so the sand is pushed into the bottom of the bucket and packed down well. It must be compacted, otherwise the castle will collapse when you remove the bucket. Scrape off the top of the sand to give a smooth level.

And now comes the exciting bit. Choose the right site for your castle – it's frustrating for everyone if you build a beautiful sandcastle in a busy part of the beach because it could easily be kicked over accidentally. Smooth down the sand on your chosen patch of beach, then invert the bucket on to the sand with a great wallop as quickly as possible. Give the base a few smart taps with the back of the spade, then gently lift off the bucket. With luck, you will reveal a wonderful sandcastle. If you aren't so lucky, just scrape up the sand and try again.

When you've produced the perfect sandcastle – or possibly a collection of them in different sizes – you can have fun decorating it with whatever takes your fancy. Create a fort with a palisade of lolly sticks (such a good excuse to eat more than one ice cream), turn your sandcastle into a sea palace with shells and trails of seaweed or recapture beach holidays of old by planting a flag on top of the castle.

Don't despair if you don't have a bucket. You can create your own free-form castle by scooping up sand and patting it into the required shape. This can be a lot more fun than creating perfect sandcastles, especially if yours tend to collapse in a heap the moment you turn your back.

If you're feeling competitive, stage a competition with your fellow beach-dwellers to see who creates the most beautiful sandcastle and whose edifice is the first to be demolished by the tide as it starts to creep back up the beach.

Sand Sculptures

If you've had enough of making sandcastles with a bucket and spade, you can raise your skills to another level by creating your own sand sculptures. You can make almost anything, from a seashell to a mermaid. You can create much larger sandcastles, too, than you would ever make with a bucket. And you might even fancy building a boat out of sand. All you need is plenty of damp sand (the same rules apply to this as to the type of sand needed for sandcastles), a spade and some patience.

Dig up masses of sand, find a smooth patch of beach away from the sea and begin patting the sand into your required shape. Decorate your finished article with pebbles, shells, seaweed or anything else that you can find. You can draw on it with the edge of a shell, or use your fingers. If there are lots of people involved, you could have a competition to see who's created the best sand sculpture. Award an ice cream as first prize.

An alternative is to draw pictures in the sand. All you need for this is the tip of a spade or a pointed pebble. Draw your name, write a message (better make sure it's polite, though) or create a wonderful seascape. The only limit is your imagination.

GETTING UP AN APPETITE

As she wheeled her wheelbarrow through streets
    broad and narrow
Crying 'Cockles and mussels! Alive, alive, oh!'

'MOLLY MALONE', JAMES YORKSTON

A Stick of Rock

If you're visiting a seaside resort and are looking for some presents to take home with you, a classic choice is a stick of rock. This is not something that you've hewn from the side of the nearest cliff but a piece of confectionery that has been a traditional feature of the seaside for many years. It was originally sold at fairgrounds but made a very successful transition to seaside resorts, with Blackpool and Morecambe the first places to literally stamp their name all the way through it. Seaside rock was especially popular, up and down the country, in the 1950s and 1960s.

Seaside rock is made from a mixture of sugar and glucose, often flavoured with peppermint, and given a colourful exterior. The piece de résistance, which reminds you that you've been to a particular resort, is that town's name running through the middle of the rock. You can't help wondering how it got there.

In a world where so many things are made by machine these days, it's reassuring to know that seaside rock is still made by hand. It's the province of a sugar boiler, and it's a skilled job. The sugar boiler heats up a huge copper vat of sugar and glucose until it reaches the desired temperature. The sticky mixture, known as toffee, is then divided in two. One half is taken to a machine where it is aerated and flavoured, and the other half is coloured using food dyes. Now it's time to create the lettering that will run through the middle of the finished stick of rock.

As with every other part of the process, this is done by hand. The individual letters are created from long strips of coloured and plain toffee. These are assembled in layers. They may not look recognisable when viewed from above, but it is easy to make out each individual letter when you look at their ends.

Now the toffee that will form the centre of the rock is placed on top of the strips of lettering. At this stage, it looks like a gigantic toffee pillowcase. This is wrapped in the coloured toffee that will form the exterior of the rock. It still bears absolutely no resemblance to the finished product at this point.

The huge toffee sausage is transferred to a machine called a batch roller, which pulls it until it is extruded in a long narrow strip. This is cut into equal lengths, which are then wrapped by hand in cellophane and labelled.

If you don't fancy a stick of rock, many seaside resorts have sweet shops that sell all sorts of objects made from sugar. They can range from lurid sets of false teeth to what look like pebbles. The perfect purchase for the traditional seaside holiday!

A PERFECT SEASIDE PICNIC

Beaches being what they are, you need to prepare in advance for an old-fashioned seaside picnic. Forget about grabbing a sandwich from the nearest shop as you rush towards the beach. This is an occasion to be planned in advance and savoured. And, ideally, you should choose plenty of traditional British food to take with you. If you can pack it in a wicker hamper, so much the better.

A tablecloth is a must, to stop sand, dead bits of seaweed, broken shells and discarded lolly sticks getting everywhere. Spread out the cloth on the sand or the pebbles, and weigh down the corners with heavy stones to prevent them flapping in the breeze that will inevitably spring up the moment you start thinking about food. It's also advisable to bring a damp flannel so everyone can wipe their fingers before and after they've eaten. If you don't do this, everything will become slightly crunchy from all that sand and you will finally understand how sandwiches got their name. You also need many more paper napkins than you might imagine, as well as some carrier bags in which you can take home all your rubbish.

When preparing everything for your picnic, bear in mind that sea air can make you incredibly hungry. It will also make you very thirsty, even if it's not particularly sunny, so always take plenty of liquids. Alcohol is not ideal because it will increase the possibility of getting dehydrated, and it can also make people behave in ways that are silly at best and dangerous at worst. Highly sugared drinks could make you more thirsty than ever, so remember to take some chilled water too.

As well as stirring up the appetite, sea air can be quite chilly, so it's a good idea to bring something hot to drink, whether it's a thermos of tea, coffee or home-made soup. If you don't want to lug lots of cutlery to the beach, pack food that's easily eaten with your fingers. If the weather is boiling hot, you'll need a cool bag to stop the food getting overheated. No matter how hungry you are, limp, warm and soggy sandwiches rapidly lose their appeal. Food poisoning isn't a good idea either, so avoid leaving the food in a hot car for hours before eating it. It's a wise move to hold back some food for later in the day because it's quite possible that you'll get hungry all over again.

Although it's lovely to have a seaside picnic on a hot summer's day, an out-of-season picnic can be just as enjoyable and you're much more likely to have the beach to yourself. But you'll have to wrap up well and take some warming food.

❧ Picnics for sunny days ❧

Scotch eggs
Mini pork pies
Egg and cress sandwiches
Ham, mustard and lettuce rolls

Chicken legs
Slices of cheese and onion quiche
Cherry tomatoes
Cucumber sticks
Grapes
Slices of cake
Home-made lemonade

❧ Picnics for cold days ❧

Thermos of hot tomato soup
Thermos of hot chicken and mushroom soup
Cornish pasties
Cold sausages
Cheese and pickle wholemeal rolls
Cornish heavy cake
Flapjacks
Chocolate cupcakes
Coffee or tea

FISH AND CHIPS

What could be nicer than spending a day on the beach and then, tired and hungry, stopping off for fish and chips on the way home? There is a theory that they taste best of all when eaten al fresco, straight from the paper with your fingers, and liberally sprinkled with salt and malt vinegar.

You might imagine that fish and chips have been a staple part of the British diet ever since the humble spud first made its appearance in the late Elizabethan era, courtesy of Sir Walter Raleigh. But it seems that until around the 1850s no one had hit on the commercial production of what has since become the classic pairing of fish and potatoes. There is some dispute about who set up the first fish and chip shop in Britain. It could have been Joseph Malin, a Jewish immigrant from Eastern Europe who opened a shop in the East End of London in 1860. Alternatively, it might have been John Lees in Oldham, Lancashire, who apparently sold fish and chips from a market stall before opening his shop in 1863. Whoever started the tradition, it caught on quickly. There were more than 30,000 fish and chip shops (often known as 'chippies') by the early 1900s.

Interestingly, Charles Dickens mentions a 'fried fish warehouse' in *Oliver Twist*, which he wrote in 1838. He also describes 'husky chips of potatoes' in *A Tale of Two Cities* (1859). What he didn't mention was that for many years the all-pervading smell of a chippie was considered to be a public nuisance. But smell or no smell, chippies were tremendously popular during the Second World War because at a time when so much food was rationed, you could buy fish and chips without using any precious food coupons. As the *Economist* magazine put it in 1940, 'The fish and chips sellers have been blessed by the Ministry of Food.'

So does all this mean that the chip, whose fame has now spread all over the world, originated in Britain? Almost certainly not. There is a story, probably apocryphal, that it was a 17th-century Belgian housewife who first cut up potatoes and flung them into hot fat. It is said that she cut them into the shape of fish, in the hope that this would fool her family into thinking they were eating more than just a plate of potatoes. Fish. And chips. Perhaps she was on to something.

Killing with Kindness

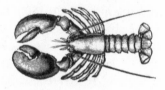

It's one thing to eat a lobster that someone else – preferably a chef – has cooked for you. It's an entirely different matter to take home a live one, and then kill it and eat it. After all, lobsters look so ferocious. You may wonder why their claws are tied together, in which case you might be unnerved to know that it's to stop them eating one another or having a go at you. And how exactly do you send a lobster off to the next world in a humane manner?

There has been a lot of debate in recent years about the kindest way to kill a lobster. Traditionally, you do it by plunging it into a large saucepan of boiling water, but that can be a harrowing experience for both you and the lobster. Eventually, with luck, the lobster won't know anything more about it but you might be haunted by the memory of it trying to climb out of the saucepan (clamp on the lid tight) or the sound of what's known as the lobster screaming. Mercifully, and as far as we know, this isn't the lobster yelling in protest at what's happening. Instead, it is the sound of air escaping from its shell, rather like the whistle of steam escaping from an old-fashioned kettle. Another option is to slit the lobster in half lengthwise. But this takes nerve, as you've got to cope with the claws waving about, and also a very sharp knife. Another option is to stab the creature through the brain. However, a lobster's brain operates from several different places, so there is no guarantee that you will have successfully killed or even stunned it.

The current theory is that the best way to kill a lobster is to put it in the freezer for about 20 minutes to reduce its core temperature and slow down its metabolism. With luck, this means it won't know anything about what happens next, which is when you cook it in your preferred manner.

Trainee chefs in restaurant kitchens are often presented with yet another problem. Many live lobsters have rather attractive blue-black shells, and the trainees are instructed to cook the lobsters without letting their shells turn red. Much to their dismay, no matter how many lobsters they cook and no matter how they cook them, the shells stubbornly continue to turn a lovely pinky-red. The reason is that a lobster shell contains many colours, including the molecules of the red astaxanthin pigment. While the lobster is alive, these molecules are contained within chains of dark protein, so aren't visible. When the lobster is cooked, these protein chains uncoil, thereby releasing the red pigment. So lo and behold, the lobster turns red. And a trainee chef's face often turns the same colour when they discover they've been the victim of an age-old culinary tease.

CORNISH HEAVY CAKE

A lthough this is called a cake, it's more like enriched pastry. It is one of Cornwall's many regional recipes and was traditionally baked for fishermen in the Truro area. These were fishermen who caught pilchards using seine nets.

There are several stories about how the cake got its name. According to one story, which seems hard to believe, the fishermen's wives would stand on a piece of high ground watching them work. When their menfolk shouted, 'Heave' as they pulled on the nets to haul them on to the boat, it was the wives' cue to disappear into their homes and bake a heavy cake to greet them on their safe return. But did these women really have nothing else to do but stand and watch their men?

Another story is that the pilchard fishermen had a look-out, known as a huer, stationed on high ground who would alert the fishermen to the shoals of pilchards by shouting, 'Hevva! Hevva!' It was hearing this cry that told the fishermen's wives that their husbands had a catch and would soon be home.

Either way, heavy cake is good with a cup of tea, and even better if you spread it with clotted cream. Cornish, of course.

The lattice pattern on the top of the cake represents the fishermen's nets.

1 lb (450 g) plain flour
8 oz (225 g) butter, cut into dice
4 oz (110 g) lard, cut into dice
Pinch of salt
6 oz (175 g) currants
2 oz (50g) candied peel
Milk
Golden caster sugar

Preheat the oven to 190°C/375°F/Gas Mark 5. Sift the flour and salt into a large mixing bowl and rub in the butter and lard. Stir in the currants, sultanas and candied peel. Using the blade of a knife, stir in a little milk until the dough has a fairly soft consistency. Place it on a floured board and lightly pat it flat with your hands until it is about ½ inch thick. Score a lattice pattern on the top of the dough. Put on a greased baking sheet and bake for about 30–40 minutes. Cut it into squares while it's still hot and sprinkle with a little sugar.

POTTED SHRIMPS

This is a classic way of serving shrimps, and is delicious when served with fresh peppery watercress, a generous wedge of lemon and some decent brown bread and butter.

1 lb (450 g) peeled shrimps
6 oz (175 g) lightly salted butter

½ tsp (2.5 ml) cayenne pepper

½ tsp (2.5 ml) mace

Salt

Pepper

Gently melt the butter in a large saucepan. Stir in the cayenne pepper and mace, then add the shrimps. Season with salt and pepper. Stir well until all the shrimps are cooked. Using a slotted spoon, divide the shrimp mixture into ramekins or small pots, pressing down the mixture. Pour the butter left in the saucepan over the top of the ramekins. Leave them to chill in the fridge until needed.

THE KNICKERBOCKER IN ALL ITS GLORY

One of the great seaside treats is eating a knickerbocker glory. It used to be a staple dish of every self-respecting ice-cream parlour, and a full-colour photo of it often featured temptingly in the window. Just what you need to keep your strength up after all that swimming.

A proper knickerbocker glory is assembled in layers in a tall glass, starting with a little sliced fruit, then a scoop each of vanilla and strawberry ice cream, followed by a hefty drizzle of strawberry or peach sauce. You then start again with more fruit. When you've crammed in as much as possible, it's topped with a huge squiggle of cream and traditionally garnished with a glacé cherry and a wafer. It is eaten with an extra long spoon so you can scrape out every last scrap of ice cream. These towering confections first appeared in the 1930s and have been going strong ever since.

It's fun to make your own. You can use fresh fruit, such as raspberries or sliced strawberries, tinned single fruits, such as sliced cling peaches, or you could choose a tinned fruit cocktail to properly evoke the spirit of the 1950s. The fruit sauce can come out of a bottle or you can make your own. When assembling the knickerbocker glory, you can be as restrained or as indulgent as you like. However, if you can manage to eat two at one sitting you probably haven't made them properly.

FLAPJACKS

L arking around on the beach and swimming in the sea can make you very hungry. These flapjacks are just the thing to help keep up your energy levels and you can also tell yourself that the addition of the muesli makes them healthy snacks. If you don't like muesli, or don't have any, leave it out but double the amount of porridge oats. Don't stint on the quality of the ingredients, as decent butter, sugar and oats make all the difference to this recipe. The only snag is that it's horribly easy to eat the lot in one go.

6 oz (175 g) butter
6 oz (175 g) light Muscovado sugar
4 oz (110 g) porridge oats
4 oz (110 g) fruit and nut muesli

Heat the oven to 220°C/425°F/Gas Mark 7. Grease a shallow 20-cm (8-in) square non-stick cake tin. Place the butter and sugar in a large heavy saucepan and gently stir over a low heat until they've completely melted. Take off the heat. Stir in the oats and the muesli until they're thoroughly coated. Turn out into the cake tin, pushing the mixture into the corners with a wooden spoon. Press it down to make the mixture compact.

Bake in the centre of the oven for about 15 minutes or until the flapjack mixture has started to turn golden brown. It will smell deliciously of toffee by this stage. Take it out of the oven before it's set as it will continue to cook in the tin. If you leave it in the oven for too long it will set too hard and endanger your fillings.

Leave to cool in the tin for about five minutes, then cut it into slices without damaging the base of the tin. Leave the tin on a wire cooling rack until the flapjack has set. Carefully lift out the slices and store in an airtight container. Unless you feel compelled to eat them straightaway!

THE REAL ZING

Having fun on a beach can be hot and thirsty work, especially on the days when the sun is blazing down, a gentle breeze is blowing and you're becoming a dab hand at making sandcastles. Some refreshment is needed, urgently, and a glass of real lemonade hits the spot in a way that few other drinks can. It has almost magical thirst-quenching powers.

Lemons can vary in tartness so it's a good idea to test the sweetness of the lemonade before you take it to the beach, adding more sugar if necessary. You want it to strike exactly the right balance between being mouth-puckeringly bitter and horribly sweet.

Transport the lemonade in a vacuum flask to keep it chilled. If you fancy having an elegant picnic you can pack some fresh mint leaves and drop them into each glass. Delicious!

This may seem like a summer drink but it's also perfect in the winter if you've got a bad cold.

6 unwaxed lemons

10 oz (250 g) granulated sugar

1¾ pints (1 litre) water

Ice cubes

Mint leaves to garnish

Scrub the lemons in hot water, then cut into small chunks. Don't worry about removing the pips at this stage. Place the lemons in a blender, tip in about half the sugar, a handful of ice cubes and half the water. Blitz for a couple of minutes. Strain the liquid through a sieve into a large wide-necked jug.

Scrape the lemon purée from the sieve back into the blender. Add the rest of the sugar and water, and some more ice cubes, then blitz again. Strain this second batch of lemonade into the jug. Discard the lemon pulp.

Taste the lemonade to see if it's sweet enough. If it isn't, put some more sugar in a bowl, pour on boiling water and let it dissolve, leave to cool and then add it to the lemonade.

To Make a Nice Whet Before Dinner

This is a recipe from Elizabeth Raffald's cookery book, *The Experienced English Housekeeper*, which was first published in 1769. As its name suggests, she recommended it as a tempting appetiser but it is equally good as a light supper.

Fry some slices of bread, half an inch thick, in butter. Lay an anchovy fillet on each one. Cover thickly with Cheshire cheese, grated and mixed with some chopped parsley. Dribble melted butter over the top and put under a hot grill until brown.

Getting in a Laver

Although Japan is the country most commonly associated with eating seaweed, this highly nutritious seafood is also a part of the traditional Welsh diet. And in both cases, purple laver (*Porphyra laciniata* or *P. umbilicalis*) is the seaweed in question. It grows along the west coast of Britain and the east coast of Ireland, and it's thought to have been eaten in Wales since medieval times.

After the laver is picked it is washed repeatedly in fresh water to get rid of every last grain of sand. Then it's boiled for several hours until it forms a thick green mushy paste. A simple way of eating it is to serve it with melted butter and some lemon juice and to eat it with bacon.

Laverbread is a Welsh speciality known as Bara Lafwr. After the laver has been boiled, it's minced and shaped into cakes that can be rolled in oatmeal or left as they are. Then these are fried and traditionally eaten for breakfast with bacon and cockles. The cockles are also a local speciality and are harvested from a small number of licensed cockle beds on the Gower Peninsula.

SEA GREENS

The British seashore offers many delicacies, but we tend to imagine that most of them are of the fishy variety. So it may come as a surprise to know that one plant, commonly found on beaches and in salt marshes, is a prized delicacy on a par with asparagus, which it resembles. This is marsh samphire (*Salicornia europaea*), also known as glasswort. Canny Britons have been eating it for centuries, whether they've picked it themselves in July and August when it's at its best, or have bought it from their fishmonger because it's the perfect partner for locally caught fish.

If you are lucky enough to find a crop of it growing naturally, you should pick the stems but leave the fibrous roots intact to produce next year's crop. After washing it thoroughly in cold water, samphire is delicious when lightly steamed and served with melted unsalted butter. It already has a salty flavour, thanks to its growing conditions, so it's not a good idea to add any more salt.

Samphire gets its name from the French *herbe de St-Pierre*. St Peter is the patron saint of fishermen, and his name means 'rock'.

One form of samphire, known as rock samphire (*Crithmum maritimum*), grows on ledges on the sides of cliffs, so picking it has always been a precarious business. The dangers of this are mentioned in Shakespeare's *King Lear*:

> 'Halfway down
> Hangs one that gathers samphire; dreadful trade!'

There was a thriving trade in picking rock samphire and gulls' eggs (the latter activity is now illegal) on the towering cliffs of the Isle of Wight in the 17th century, and in 1664 Robert Turner expressed his thoughts about it in his book *Botonologia: The British Physician*: 'It is incredibly dangerous to gather; yet many adventure it, though they buy their sauce with the price of their lives.'

SOME SCRUMPTIOUS SHELLFISH

These days, Britain imports seafood from all over the world. Yet there is a rich variety of shellfish alone that is native to the British Isles. Long before the days of supermarkets and the cost of food miles, local communities ate local food. And coastal communities had the pick of a wide variety of seafood and shellfish that were valued for being plentiful, delicious and which provided a good source of protein.

Here are some of the edible shellfish that populate the British coastal waters.

COCKLES

As we are often reminded, small can be beautiful. And that's certainly true in the case of cockles. These edible saltwater clams grow in many parts of the world but do particularly well in the British Isles, where they are traditionally raked out of the sands of sheltered beaches a couple of hours after the tide has gone out. You will find one of three types of cockle: the common cockle (*Cerastoderma edule*), the prickly cockle (*Acanthocardia echinata*) and the lagoon cockle (*Cerastoderma glaucum*). The common cockle has a nifty trick for escaping predators – it can jump.

Cockles are good to eat all year round. They can be eaten raw but are traditionally boiled, then seasoned with malt vinegar and white pepper.

MUSSELS

The common mussel (*Mytilus edulis*) grows abundantly around the British coastline, and has been eaten for hundreds of years. It can be eaten throughout the year. Fresh mussels should always be bought when they are still alive, with their shells closed, as they will start to decay quickly once they've died. They must be scrubbed in clean water to remove their beards (the bit that enables them to hold on to the surface on which they grow in the sea). Classic ways of cooking them include steaming in a hot pan and cooking in a garlicky sauce. Any mussels that fail to open their shells at this point must be discarded because they aren't safe to eat.

OYSTERS

How times have changed. Today, oysters are a delicacy and a luxury. But in Victorian times they were eaten by the rich and poor alike.

Before the Romans arrived in Britain, shellfish was considered to be something that you ate when times were hard and you couldn't find anything better. But the Romans thought differently. Apparently, they either had such a high opinion of Britain's native oysters, or such a low opinion of the country (it depends which way you look at it), that they claimed oysters were the best thing they found in Britain.

Oyster consumption dropped again once the Romans decamped back to mainland Europe but began to rise in the late 8th century. By the 15th century, oysters were eaten by all classes in Britain. They were so plentiful and cheap that large oysters were used to bulk up dishes when meat was scarce, hence the steak and oyster pie. Small oysters were eaten raw. They were just as popular during Victorian times but the combination of the two world wars, harsh winters and food contamination scares dealt a severe blow to the oyster industry in the 20th century.

Today, two sorts of oysters are grown and sold in Britain – native oysters (*Ostrea edulis*) and Pacific, or rock, oysters (*Crassostrea gigas*), which originated in the Pacific Ocean. Native oysters spawn for part of the year and are best eaten between September and April (famously, when there is an 'R' in the month), while rock oysters can be eaten throughout the year. Several towns, areas and counties are famous for their oysters, including Whitstable in Kent; the Camel and Fal Estuaries in Cornwall; Milford Haven in Wales; Colchester in Essex; Loch Fyne and Loch Ryan in Scotland; Galway in Ireland, and many more.

SHRIMPS

The common or brown shrimp (*Crangon crangon*) lives in bays and inlets, only coming out to feed at night. While some native shellfish, such as whelks and winkles, are often ignored, shrimps are very popular. Although you can catch them with a shrimping net (which is what the fictional Jeeves used to do on his holidays from his employer, Bertie Wooster), it is difficult to spot them because they are highly skilled at changing their appearance to match their surroundings. Which only goes to prove how clever Jeeves was.

WHELKS

The common whelk (*Buccinum undatum*) is a form of snail, but don't let that put you off eating it. It lives on the seabed, where it gets around using its one large black and white spotted foot which is propelled along by waves of its muscles.

Fishermen catch whelks using a small type of lobster pot that they bait with pieces of fish or crab. Whelks are cleaned in several changes of fresh water, then boiled for between 10–15 minutes in salted water. They are usually sprinkled with malt vinegar. Although they're available throughout the year, they're at their best between September and February.

WINKLES

Winkles are a form of snail. They are also known as the common periwinkle (*Littorina littorea*), as well as willicks or wilks in some parts of the country, and they are found around the British coastline but particularly along the coasts of Scotland and Ireland. These tiny shellfish have been eaten for centuries and have been a part of the Scottish diet since at least 7500 BC. Like their much larger cousins, whelks, they are high in protein. They should be bought when still alive, washed in two changes of fresh water and then boiled for a couple of minutes. They are winkled out of their shells with pins or toothpicks.

COASTAL LIFE

The sun was shining on the sea
Shining with all its might
He did his very best to make
The billows smooth and bright –
And this was odd because it was
The middle of the night.

ALICE THROUGH THE LOOKING GLASS, LEWIS CARROLL

Searching for Shells

Britain's coastlines are rich in shells. On some beaches you can find thousands of them scattered over the shoreline every time the tide goes out. Many of the shells are broken because they are in the process of being smashed up by the waves, but you will also spot intact shells. Here are some of the species you can expect to find.

Alder's necklace shell (*Euspira pulchella*)
American oyster (*Crassostrea virginica*)
American oyster drill (*Urosalpinx cinerea*)
American piddock (*Petricola pholadiformis*)
Arctic cowrie (*Trivia arctica*)
Atlantic surf clam (*Spisula solidissima*)
Auger shell (*Turritella communis*)
Baltic tellin (*Macoma balthica*)
Banded chink shell (*Lacuna vincta*)
Banded venus (*Clausinella fasciata*)
Banded wedge shell (*Donax vittatus*)
Basket shell (*Corbula gibba*)
Bean-like tellin (*Fabulina fabula*)
Bearded mussel (*Modiolus barbatus*)
Black-footed limpet (*Patella depressa*)

Blue-rayed limpet (*Helcion pellucidum*)
Blunt gaper (*Mya truncata*)
Chequered carpet shell (*Ruditapes decussatus*)
China limpet (*Patella ulyssiponensis*)
Chinaman's hat (*Calyptraea chinensis*)
Common cockle (*Cerastoderma edule*)

Common cuttlefish (*Sepia officinalis*)
Common flat periwinkle (*Littorina obtusata*)
Common keyhole limpet (*Diodora graeca*)
Common limpet (*Patella vulgata*)
Common mussel (*Mytilus edulis*)
Common otter shell (*Lutraria lutraria*)
Common pelican's foot (*Aporrhais pespelecani*)
Common periwinkle (*Littorina littorea*)
Common piddock (*Pholas dactylus*)
Common tortoiseshell limpet (*Tectura testudinalis*)
Common wentletrap (*Epitonium clathrus*)
Common whelk (*Buccinum undatum*)
Curved razor shell (*Ensis ensis*)
DeFolin's lagoon snail (*Caecum armoricum*)
Dog cockle (*Glycymeris glycymeris*)
Dog whelk (*Nucella lapillus*)
Elegant cuttlefish (*Sepia elegans*)
European cowrie (*Trivia monacha*)
Fan mussel (*Atrina pectinata*)
Flat periwinkle (*Littorina obtusata*)

Flat top shell (*Gibbula umbilicalis*)
Gaping file shell (*Limaria hians*)
Great scallop (*Pecten maximus*)
Great shipworm (*Teredo navalis*)
Green crenella (*Musculus discors*)
Green ormer (*Haliotis tuberculata*)
Grey top shell (*Gibbula cineraria*)
Grooved top shell (*Jujubinus striatus*)
Hard-shell clam (*Mercenaria mercenaria*)
Horse mussel (*Modiolus modiolus*)
Humpback scallop (*Chlamys distorta*)
Icelandic cyprine (*Arctica islandica*)
Keyhole limpet (Diodora apertura)
Lagoon cockle (*Cerastoderma glaucum*)
Lagoon snail (*Paludinella littorina*)
Large necklace shell (*Euspira catena*)
Large sunset shell (*Gari depressa*)
Laver spire shell (*Hydrobia ulvae*)

Little cuttlefish (*Sepiola atlantica*)
Lobe shell (*Philine aperta*)
Looping snail (*Truncatella subcylindrica*)
Manila clam (*Ruditapes philippinarum*)
Marbled crenella (*Modiolarca tumida*)
Native oyster (*Ostrea edulis*)
Necklace shell (*Euspira catena*)
Needle whelk (*Bittium reticulatum*)

Netted dog whelk (*Hinia reticulata*)
Northern hatchet shell (*Thyasira gouldi*)
Oval venus (*Timoclea ovata*)
Oyster drill (*Ocenebra erinacea*)
Pacific oyster (*Crassostrea gigas*)
Painted topshell (*Calliostoma zizyphinum*)
Pearly top shell (*Margarites helicinus*)
Peppery furrow shell (*Scrobicularia plana*)
Pheasant shell (*Tricolia pullus*)
Pink cuttlefish (*Sepia orbigniana*)

Pod razor shell (*Ensis siliqua*)
Pullet carpet shell (*Venerupis senegalensis*)
Purple top shell (*Gibbula umbilicalis*)
Queen scallop (*Aequipecten opercularis*)
Rayed Artemis (*Dosinia exoleta*)
Rayed trough shell (*Mactra stultorum*)
Red whelk (*Neptunea antiqua*)
Rough periwinkle (*Littorina saxatilis*)
Saddle oyster (*Anomia ephippium*)
Sand gaper (*Mya arenaria*)
Slipper limpet (*Crepidula fornicata*)
Slit limpet (*Emarginula fissura*)
Small periwinkle (*Melarhaphe neritoides*)
Smooth Artemis (*Dosinia lupinus*)
Smooth venus (*Callista chione*)

Spiny cockle (*Acanthocardia aculeata*)
Spotted cowrie (*Trivia monacha*)
Striped venus clam (*Chamelea gallina*)
Surf clam (*Spisula solida*)
Thick-lipped dog whelk (*Nassarius incrassatus*)
Thick top shell (*Osilinus lineatus*)
Thick trough shell (*Spisula solida*)
Thin tellin (*Angulus tenuis*)
Tortoiseshell limpet (*Tectura testudinalis*)
Tower shell (*Turritella communis*)
Variegated scallop (*Chlamys varia*)
Veined rapa whelk (*Rapana venosa*)
Velvet shell (*Velutina velutina*)
Violet snail (*Janthina janthina*)
Warty venus (*Venus verrucosa*)
White piddock (*Barnea candida*)
Wrinkled rock borer (*Hiatella arctica*)

SALTY TASTES

Plants can be remarkably adaptable. Although humans wouldn't survive if they were regularly flooded with seawater, some plants have adapted to their maritime conditions to such an extent that they either grow best in salty conditions or struggle to compete in a non-salty environment. Some salt marsh plants have even learnt to tell the difference between sodium and potassium.

But how do they get to these apparently inhospitable environments in the first place? If an area of land is cleared of vegetation (as a result of a landslip, volcano or a cliff fall) or it has newly emerged from the sea, we get what botanists call primary succession. This means the first species to arrive here perform a specific function that modifies the environment.

Ironically, this eventually makes it less of a choice spot for themselves, so they then give way to the next set of species, which modifies the area still further, until a steady state is reached. The pioneer plants form the soil in the first place by accumulating dust and organic debris, binding the sand or eroding the rock, locking in the carbon and nitrogen in the soil, stabilising it and drying it out, so other plants can get a foothold when they arrive. It is usually the lower plants that arrive initially after landslips, so the progression might be lichens first, then mosses and liverworts, then ferns, and finally flowering plants and trees.

In sheltered environments, the sand dunes that form often have a series of ridges. The hollows between the ridges are called 'slacks'. These are often wet, and provide the perfect habitat for marshland plants and animals. They are all kept in check by the tides.

On the coastlines of north-west Scotland and Ireland, the Atlantic waves eventually pound shells into tiny fragments, which are then incorporated into the surrounding sands. The resulting sand dunes are known as 'machair' and are home to abundant wild flowers. Where they exist between the shore and a peat bog, the alkaline sand helps to offset the acid of the bog which makes the soil in the middle nicely fertile.

Some plants that are at home in salty conditions can also survive very happily on the tops of mountains, because these are equally harsh, exposed environments with bright sunshine, plenty of wind and a lack of fresh water. These plants include scurvy grass (*Cochlearia anglica*), sea campion (*Silene maritime*), sea plantain (*Plantago maritima*) and sea thrift (*Armeria maritima*).

Interestingly, since we began sprinkling salt on our roads in the winter, some salt-tolerant plants have spread inland along our motorways. The dry air, salty conditions and rushing winds are all similar to the coastal environment.

✄ Plants that grow in salt marshes ✄

Cord grass (*Spartina* spp.)

Glasswort (*Salicornia* spp.)

Orache (*Atriplex hastata*)

Red alga (*Bostrychia scorpioides*)
Red fescue grass (*Festuca rubra*)
Salt marsh grass (*Puccinellia maritima*)
Scurvy grass (*Cochlearia* spp.)
Sea aster (*Aster tripolium*)
Seablite (*Suaeda maritima*)
Sea lavender (*Limonium humile*)
Sea milkwort (*Glaux maritima*)
Sea plantain (*Plantago maritima*)
Sea purslane (*Atriplex portulacoides*)
Sea spurrey (*Spergularia* spp.)
Sea thrift (*Armeria maritima*)

❧ Plants that grow on sand dunes ❧

Jointed rush (*Juncus articulatus*)
Marram grass (*Ammophila arenaria*)
Orache (*Atriplex* spp.)
Portland spurge (*Euphorbia portlandica*)
Prickly saltwort (*Salsola kali*)
Red fescue grass (*Festuca rubra*)
Restharrow (*Ononis repens*)
Sand couch grass (*Elytrigia juncea*)
Sand sedge (*Carex arenaria*)
Sea bindweed (*Calystegia soldanella*)
Sea holly (*Eryngium maritimum*)
Sea rocket (*Cakile maritima*)
Sea sandwort (*Honckenya peploides*)
Sea spurge (*Euphorbia paralias*)
Twisted moss (*Tortula ruralis* ssp. *ruraliformis*)

THE BUTTERFLIES FLUTTER BY

You might imagine that coastal regions of the British Isles are too harsh to attract delicate butterflies and moths, but several species are attracted to the plants that grow along the coasts, as well as on the chalk and limestone cliffs. Here are some of the butterflies and moths, and also the plants that the caterpillars feed on.

Adonis blue (*Lysandra bellargus*)	Horseshoe vetch
Brown argus (*Aricia agestis*)	Rock rose, storksbill
Chalk-hill blue (*Lysandra coridon*)	Horseshoe vetch
Cinnabar moth (*Tyria jacobaeae*)	Ragwort
Clouded yellow (*Colias crocea*)	Legumes, esp. clover
Common blue (*Polyommatus icarus*)	Legumes, esp. clover
Drinker moth (*Euthrix potatoria*)	Coarse grasses
Fiery clearwing (*Pyropteron chrysidiformis*)	Dock roots
Gatekeeper (*Pyronia tithonus*)	*Poa* and *Milium* grasses
Glanville frittilary (*Melitaea cinxia*)	Ribwort plantain
Grayling (*Hipparchia semele*)	Grasses, esp. *Festuca*
Holly blue (*Celastrina argiolus*)	Holly, dogwood, ivy
Hummingbird hawk-moth (*Macroglossum stellatarum*)	Bedstraw
Large blue (*Maculinea arion*)	Wild thyme
Large skipper (*Ochlodes venatus*)	Grasses

Large white (*Pieris brassicae*)	Brassicas
Marbled white (*Melanargia galathea*)	Grasses
Mazarine blue (*Cyaniris semiargus*)	Clover, kidney vetch
Meadow brown (*Maniola jurtina*)	Grasses, esp. *Poa*
Peacock butterfly (*Inachis io*)	Nettles
Ringlet (*Aphantopus hyperantus*)	Grasses
Scarlet tiger moth (*Callimorpha dominula*)	Comfrey, hemp agrimony, hound's tongue
Short-tailed blue (*Everes argiades*)	Medick, trefoil
Silver-spotted skipper (*Hesperia comma*)	Grasses
Silver-studded blue (*Plebejus argus*)	Gorse, broom
Six-spot burnet (*Zygaena filipendulae*)	Bird's-foot trefoil
Small (or little) blue (*Cupido minimus*)	Kidney vetch
Small copper (*Lycaena phlaeas*)	Dock, sorrel
Small heath (*Coenonympha pamphilus*)	Grasses
Small white (*Artogeia rapae*)	Wild mignonette, brassicas
Transparent burnet (*Zygaena purpuralis*)	Wild thyme
Wall brown (*Lasiommata megera*)	Grasses, esp. *Poa*

A WORD IN YOUR SHELL-LIKE

One of the many joys of being a child – of whatever age – is holding a seashell close to your ear so you can hear the sea. It works every time, whether you're in a town or by the seaside, provided that the shell is big enough to fit around your ear. And, unless your ears deceive you, the age-old sound of the sea murmuring against the shore has been captured in every shell. Magical, isn't it?

Science has a different explanation. Rather than the essence of the sea being captured inside the shell in a way that defies logic but which captivates the imagination, it's much more likely that the sound emanating from the shell is part of the ambient noise around you. This means that it's hard to hear any noise in the shell if you're in a quiet room. But if you're in a noisy environment, the noise inside the shell will be quite loud.

Alternatively, you may prefer to believe that the sound of the waves simply has to be louder in order to compete with the noise of your surroundings.

IN A CRABBY MOOD

One of the great comic images of the seaside is an unsuspecting bather wincing because a crab's pinchers are clutched tightly round one of their toes. Happily for most bathers, this is a rather dramatic piece of poetic licence because crabs are usually quite shy creatures, preferring to scuttle away at the first hint of human intrusion rather than clamp themselves to the nearest piece of succulent flesh while it's still moving. They hide under rocks, stones and seaweed – anything to keep out of your way.

Crabs are scavengers, which makes them very useful members of the seashore. Their idea of a delicious meal is to gobble up any dead plants or animals they can find, ranging from the minute plants known collectively as plankton to dead fish. They might even have a nibble of your discarded ham sandwich.

Because crabs are hard-shelled creatures, they look as though their soft inner bodies are perfectly defended against the rest of the world. However, they have an inherent problem: their shells don't grow but their bodies do. This means that every crab periodically has to slough off its old shell in a process known as moulting, and hide while it grows a new one. A crab's new shell will already have started growing before it loses the old one, but even so it must allow time for the shell to harden. Otherwise, it runs the risk of becoming a delicious meal for whichever predator happens to be passing.

Crabs are born with ten legs, which include two very strong claws that they use to fight other crabs and catch food. They have the very clever ability to discard a leg if it's been grabbed by a predator and they want to escape. Each leg has a special breaking point at which it can part company with the crab's body without causing excessive bleeding. The leg begins to grow back during successive moults until it eventually reaches its original size. Assuming, of course, that it hasn't been detached again in the meantime.

What sort of crabs might you expect to see on British beaches? There are quite a few, including four that are very common.

✌ Edible crab (*Cancer pagurus*) ✌

This is easy to identify if you've seen one on a fishmonger's slab. The broad and oval shell is bright orange, and it has very long claws with black tips. Although you might be tempted to take one home for supper when you spot it on the beach, it is against the law to catch these crabs unless you are licensed to do so.

✎ Hairy crab (*Pilumnus hirtellus*) ✎

The hairy crab looks quite similar to the edible crab, but its orange shell and legs are covered with tiny hairs – hence its name. Its two claws are always of different sizes.

✎ Shore crab (*Carcinus maenas*) ✎

This is one of the most common crabs, and you can see shore crabs in a variety of colours from brown to green to orange. They range from being tiny to quite a decent size. You are most likely to see them in shallow waters and in rock pools. All their legs are pointed, to enable them to cling on to rocks.

✎ Velvet swimming crab (*Necora puber*) ✎

Another very common crab around the British coastline, this gets its name from the tiny hairs on its shell that give it a velvety appearance. However, its behaviour is far from velvety because it will give you a sharp nip with its claws if you get too close. Other crabs are wary of it, too, because it will happily eat them. Its rear legs are flattened to help it to swim.

Other British crabs include the masked crab (*Corystes cassivelaunus*), which has a tube between its antennae to help it to breathe, and the pea crab (*Pinnotheres pisum*), whose brown male is tiny and whose yellow female is twice the size and spends her entire life inside a live mussel shell.

CLINGING ON LIKE A LIMPET

According to popular sayings, nothing clings on as tightly as a limpet. We talk of someone clinging on like a limpet when they won't let go of something, whether it's a possession or a relationship. In warfare, a particular type of underwater mine that is fixed to a ship's hull is called a limpet mine, because it adheres to the ship's bottom until it detonates. So you might be forgiven for assuming that limpets also hold on tight to things and never let go. But you would be wrong.

In fact, limpets – the small creatures that live in tent-shaped shells – like to go for a wander every now and then. They visit other rocks before returning to their own rocky abode. They clamp themselves to a stone whenever they can feel vibrations around them, but when all is calm they sit with their shells slightly raised. It's at this point that you can pick them up. Despite looking like such peaceful – not to mention inert – creatures, they can get involved in battles for the perfect position on a rock, and might even flick one another over in order to get the upper hand, so to speak.

It's barnacles that stay in one place throughout their lives. They begin their search for their perfect home when they are still larvae, and when they've found their ideal rock they attach themselves to it with a form of cement that they secrete. They then develop into their adult form, complete with shell. And there they stay, on their favoured rock, for the rest of their days, using their legs to catch food as it drifts past. Not a particularly exciting life, you might imagine. But then, not being barnacles, who are we to say?

BEACHCOMBING

One of the great pleasures of being on a beach is strolling along and seeing what you can find. The tide washes up all sorts of treasures, whether animal, vegetable or mineral. Shells and seaweed are self-explanatory, but some of the other things you can find on a beach look very strange, making it almost impossible to guess what they are.

❦ Cuttlefish ❦

Some people only know of cuttlefish (*Sepia* spp.) because they give the bones to their budgies to peck for the calcium they contain, but a walk along the seashore can also show you some cuttlefish bones. These are beautifully white and smooth. They are porous and give the cuttlefish buoyancy, which is why they are washed ashore after the cuttlefish dies and its flesh either rots or is eaten. Each species of cuttlefish has a distinctive shape and size of cuttlebone, as it's called.

❦ Lugworm casts ❦

Every time the tide goes out the wet beach can be covered in what look like small coils of sand. These are the casts of the lugworm

(*Arenicola marina*), also known as the sandworm. It spends its life in a U-shaped burrow in the sand, and the cast that appears above its home is the material it defecates after feeding. Normally, you will never see the worm itself, unless you are an angler who's digging up lugworms to use as fishing bait. Very occasionally, you might see a bird pulling the lugworm to the surface and eating it.

∽ Mermaid's purse ∽

It's easy to see why this got its name because it looks like a purse made out of a waterproof fabric, with ribbons flowing from either end. Alternatively, you might think it resembles a burst balloon, with both ends open. In fact, it's the empty egg capsule of the lesser-spotted dogfish (*Scyliorhinus canicula*). The eggs within this capsule take between five and eleven months to hatch, depending on the water temperature. However, when they are washed up on the seashore any eggs that are left inside the capsule are almost certainly doomed.

∽ Sea potato tests ∽

The sea potato (*Echinocardium cordatum*) is a type of sea urchin that lives just below the surface of the sand. It's covered in so many brown spines that it looks as though it's covered in fur. But when it dies, the spines break off to leave a white, hard skeleton (also known as a 'test') that is often seen on the seashore.

∽ Sea urchin tests ∽

When they're alive, sea urchins have hundreds of long, poisonous spines that wave about in the sea to trap the algae that they eat. When they die, the spines break off, leaving behind a hard, round test that can get washed up on the beach. These tests can vary tremendously in size from very small to quite large, and some are brightly coloured.

⟡ Shark egg cases ⟡

Some sharks lay eggs, and the empty egg cases are often washed up on the beach. These are camouflaged to look like seaweed, so they can be difficult to spot. If you're looking out for them, they are black and shiny.

⟡ Whelk egg cases ⟡

These can look very strange when you find them on the beach, and at first you might even imagine they are discarded bubblewrap. But what you are looking at is the egg case of the whelk (*Buccinum undatum*), which lays large clumps of eggs on rocks in the sea. Sometimes, especially in stormy weather, these eggs are washed up on to the shoreline. If the egg case is grey it means the eggs have already hatched and the case is empty. If it's yellow, it means that a few eggs remain.

STINGS AND THINGS

If anything on a beach should be labelled DO NOT TOUCH, it's jelly-fish. These floaty creatures can measure anything from the size of your fingernail to almost the length of your arm. Some summer visi-tors are much bigger than that. And some jellyfish are harmless while others carry a nasty sting, even when they're dead.

Jellyfish are very beautiful creatures, especially when viewed on the move in the sea. They swim using a form of jet propulsion, sucking up water into their bodies and then shooting it out again. They feed on a varied diet of plankton that they catch in the layer of mucus that covers their bodies. Tiny hairs, called 'cilia', move the plankton towards the edge of the jellyfish 'bell', at which point the jellyfish picks up the food with its arms and pops it in its mouth. It can also eat small fish, which it catches with the help of its stinging tentacles.

Two species of jellyfish live around the coasts of Britain. The common, or moon, jellyfish (*Aurelia aurita*) is easily identified, thanks to its four crescent moon-shaped tissues on the underside of its violet-tinged body. It is harmless to humans. The compass jellyfish (*Chrysaora hyoscella*) is washed on to beaches in the summer, especially in the southern part of Britain. It is orangey-brown, with 32 lobes that look like brown stripes.

Other species sometimes get washed up on British shores or are seen in British waters. These are the jellyfish that should be approached with caution, as several of them carry powerful stings. The biggest of the lot is lion's mane jellyfish (*Cyanea capillata*), which has the potential to grow up to six feet (two metres) in diameter although most of these creatures are of much more modest proportions. They get their name from their long trails of sticky tentacles which can deliver quite a strong string. Barrel jellyfish (*Rhizostoma octopus*), which are up to three feet (one metre) long, have been appearing around the Welsh coast in increasing numbers over recent years. They have eight tentacles but are harmless to humans, despite their menacing appearance. Blue jellyfish (*Cyanea lamarckii*) look quite similar to the lion's mane jellyfish, but are smaller. They carry a mild sting. Keep away from the mauve stinger (*Pelagia noctiluca*), which is small and, as its name suggests, is mauve and a stinger.

Be especially wary of the Portuguese man-of-war (*Physalia physalia*). It isn't a true jellyfish because it consists of colonies of tiny creatures called hydrozoans. It's blue-purple, oval and has trailing tentacles that can be massively long and which deliver a very nasty sting. These jelly-like creatures like to swarm in huge numbers, making them a highly dangerous proposition for anything – or anyone – that gets in their way. They normally live far out in the oceans but winds or currents can occasionally wash them up on to the beach, where they should be treated with extreme caution. In some cases, their presence on the sand means the entire beach has to be closed until they've been safely removed.

SEAWARD FOR SEAWEED

If you go down to the beach today you're almost certain to spot some seaweed, especially if it's low tide. Yet even at high tide you'll probably find some strands of seaweed that have been washed on to the beach, especially after some rough weather. There are fewer seaweeds in areas with fast currents, and also fewer around sewage outlets because of the silty sea floor and the lack of clarity in the water.

If you're a phycologist (which means you study algae), you will already go into raptures about the different types of seaweed that can be found on British coasts. If you aren't, you may regard seaweed as slippery, slimy stuff that gives you the creeps. But there's a lot more to it than that. For instance, you can tell the age of one common seaweed simply by counting the number of bladders on its fronds. Seaweed provides shelter and food for many marine creatures, including limpets which are one of its main predators.

'Seaweed' is the collective noun for many different species of large marine algae that live on seashores and in shallow seas. They fall into three categories: green (Chlorophyta), red (Rhodophyta) and brown

(Phaeophyta) algae. Their colours are caused by pigments which differ widely but they are all used in photosynthesis (the conversion of sunlight into sugar). Land-based plants have leaves, whereas seaweeds have fronds, and it's these that enable you to identify the different varieties. You'll find different seaweeds in different areas of the beach.

❧ Seaweeds found high on the beach ❧

These include the brown seaweeds. They have an outer mucilaginous layer that absorbs water, so when they're out of water it's this layer that dries out rather than their internal cells. Seaweeds are always attached to something, such as a rock, with a base (sometimes disc-shaped, sometimes root-like or claw-like) called a holdfast.

CHANNELLED WRACK (*Pelvetia canaliculata*) You'll find this high up on the beach, where it can survive for several days with only sea spray for moisture. The fronds are rolled lengthwise, hence the name of this seaweed. It turns black when it's very dry. It can lose 80 per cent of its water when out of the sea but it will recover in minutes once it's submerged again.

SPIRAL WRACK (*Fucus spiralis*) This has flat, straight-edged fronds with a midrib. Sometimes the fronds twist into a spiral.

❧ Seaweeds found in the middle ❧
to lower beach

This is where the green seaweeds grow, although there aren't many of these. You will often find them half in, half out of the water. They need good light, so won't be found in shadow. You will find brown seaweeds here, too.

SEA LETTUCE (*Ulva* sp.) Sea lettuce is the common name for the many different green seaweeds found in rock pools and on the lower shore. They have lettuce-like fronds, which are only a few cells thick.

GUT WEED (*Enteromorpha intestinalis*) A green seaweed with tubular fronds that look like intestines.

EGG WRACK (*Ascophyllum nodosum*) This is a brown seaweed and it grows abundantly in sheltered areas. It has long, strap-like fronds and large, single air bladders. Each frond produces one bladder a year.

BLADDER WRACK (*Fucus vesiculosus*) This brown seaweed has air bladders, often arranged in pairs, either side of the midribs, which allow it to float in the water. The more exposed the beach, the fewer bladders there will be on the bladder wrack.

Seaweeds found on the lower beach or in rock pools

You will find here the seaweeds that can't tolerate being excessively dry.

DABBERLOCKS (*Alaria esculenta*) The wonderfully named dabberlocks can grow very large. It is a brown seaweed with narrow fronds that are slightly puckered and have a midrib. It's much more common in the north of Britain than the south. It can grow in rock pools as well as the lower shore.

SUGAR KELP (*Saccharina latissima*) Another brown seaweed, this has frilly edges and looks similar to dabberlocks, except that it doesn't have a midrib. It grows on the lower shore and also in rock pools.

THONGWEED (*Himanthalia elongata*) This brown seaweed has long, narrow strap-like fronds and thrives in exposed locations. Its holdfast looks like a button mushroom.

TOOTHED WRACK (*Fucus serratus*) Toothed wrack is a brown seaweed that looks similar to spiral wrack, but its fronds have toothed edges. It grows abundantly and is one of the most common British seaweeds.

WIREWEED (*Sargassum muticum*) This brown seaweed isn't a native plant and it's becoming very invasive in southern Britain. It has many small fronds growing from a central stipe, with small round pods. You can find it in rock pools as well as on the lower shore.

BIFURCARIA BIFURCATA This brown seaweed has rounded fronds that end in forks. It is only found in south-west England and west Ireland.

CORALLINA sp. These red seaweeds are stiff, chalky and resemble coral. They are usually light pink in colour and look jointed.

GRACILARIA sp. These red seaweeds are translucent, and are dark red or brown in colour. They are used to make agar, which is a vegetarian alternative to gelatin.

STOWAWAYS AND STRANDED PLANTS

Some of the plants that now grow freely in Britain first arrived by sea. Plant collecting was wildly fashionable from the early 1600s, and as explorers discovered more parts of the world they brought back increasing numbers of the plants they found on their travels. There are stories of some of these ships being wrecked and the bulbs being washed ashore, where they liked the conditions they found and set up home. These adventurous bulbs are thought to include nerines and agapanthus.

One plant that began life in Britain only a century ago has gone on to flourish as a brand-new species. Common cordgrass (*Spartina anglica*) began life when one of its parents (*S. alternifolia*) arrived in Southampton as a stowaway (possibly travelling in a ship's ballast water). It hybridised with the native *S. maritima* and has now colonised many salt marshes and sand dunes. Unfortunately, it has become invasive and can smother other native plants, which in turn affects the local wildlife.

Other plants once grew on what are now the British Isles but then found themselves stranded abroad and couldn't get back. During the last mini Ice Age approximately 10,000 years ago, most of Britain was covered with ice. There were land bridges between England and France (which didn't entirely disappear until 8,500 years ago), and also between Scotland and Ireland. As the ice encroached from the north, the plants retreated further and further south. When the ice eventually melted, the land bridges were flooded by the English Channel and the Atlantic, so the plants were cut off and couldn't get home again. These species, which include the thistle *Ciresium oleraceum*, survive in north-west France but can't hop back over the Channel.

ALONG THE COAST

You gentlemen of England
Who live at home at ease,
How little do you think
Of the dangers of the seas.

'THE VALIANT SAILORS', MARTIN PARKER

Common Coastal Birds

The coastline is home to all manner of birds that you are unlikely to see in your garden. Some of these birds are visitors from other countries. Others might live in the UK all year round but only visit the seashore or coastal marshes at a specific time of year.

❧ Can be seen all year round ❧

Avocet (*Recurvirostra avosetta*)
Black guillemot (*Cepphus grylle*)
Black-headed gull (*Larus ridibundus*)
Black-tailed godwit (*Limosa limosa*)
Carrion crow (*Corvus corone*)
Chough (*Pyrrhocorax pyrrhocorax*)
Common gull (*Larus canus*)
Common scoter (*Melanitta nigra*)
Cormorant (*Phalacrocorax carbo*)
Curlew (*Numenius arquata*)
Dunlin (*Calidris alpina*)
Eider (*Somateria mollissima*)
Fulmar (*Fulmarus glacialis*)
Gadwall (*Anas strepera*)

Gannet (*Sula bassana*)
Goldeneye (*Bucephala clangula*)
Great black-backed gull (*Larus marinus*)
Greenshank (*Tringa nebularia*)
Grey plover (*Pluvialis squatarola*)
Knot (*Calidris canuta*)
Mediterranean gull (*Larus melanocephalus*)
Oystercatcher (*Haematopus ostralegus*)
Peregrine (*Falco peregrinus*)
Redshank (*Tringa totanus*)
Ringed plover (*Charadrius hiaticula*)
Rock dove (*Columba livia*)
Rock pipit (*Anthus petrosus*)
Ruff (*Philomachus pugnax*)
Sanderling (*Calidris alba*)
Shag (*Phalacrocorax aristotelis*)
Shelduck (*Tadorna tadorna*)
Teal (*Anas crecca*)
Turnstone (*Arenaria interpres*)
Wigeon (*Anas penelope*)
Yellow-legged gull (*Larus michahellis*)

❧ Summer visitors ❧

Aquatic warbler (*Acrocephalus paludicola*)
Arctic skua (*Stercorarius parasiticus*)
Arctic tern (*Sterna paradisaea*)
Balearic shearwater (*Puffinus mauretanicus*)
Common tern (*Sterna hirundo*)
Curlew sandpiper (*Calidris ferruginea*)
Great shearwater (*Puffinus gravis*)
Great skua (*Catharacta skua*)

Guillemot (*Uria aalge*)
Herring gull (*Larus argentatus*)
Kittiwake (*Rissa tridactyla*)
Leach's petrel (*Oceanodroma leucorhoa*)
Lesser black-backed gull (*Larus fuscus*)
Little gull (*Larus minutus*)
Little stint (*Calidris minuta*)
Little tern (*Sterna albifrons*)
Long-tailed skua (*Stercorarius longicaudus*)
Manx shearwater (*Puffinus puffinus*)
Pomarine skua (*Stercorarius pomarinus*)
Puffin (*Fratercula arctica*)
Razorbill (*Alca torda*)
Red-necked phalarope (*Phalaropus lobatus*)
Red-throated diver (*Gavia stellata*)
Roseate tern (*Sterna dougallii*)
Sandwich tern (*Sterna sandvicensis*)
Whimbrel (*Numenius phaeopus*)
Wood sandpiper (*Tringa glareola*)

❧ Winter visitors ❧

Barnacle goose (*Branta leucopsis*)
Bar-tailed godwit (*Limosa lapponica*)
Black-throated diver (*Gavia arctica*)
Brent goose (*Brant bernicla*)

Glaucous gull (*Larus hyperboreus*)
Great crested grebe (*Podiceps cristatus*)
Great grey shrike (*Lanius excubitor*)
Great northern diver (*Gavia immer*)
Grey phalarope (*Phalaropus fulicarius*)
Iceland gull (*Larus glaucoides*)
Little auk (*Alle alle*)
Little grebe (*Tachybaptus ruficollis*)
Long-tailed duck (*Clangula hyemalis*)
Purple sandpiper (*Calidris maritima*)
Red-breasted merganser (*Mergus serrator*)
Red-necked grebe (*Podiceps grisegena*)
Scaup (*Aythya marila*)
Shorelark (*Eremopila alpestris*)
Short-eared owl (*Asio flammeus*)
Slavonian grebe (*Podiceps auritus*)
Spotted redshank (*Tringa erythropus*)
Velvet scoter (*Melanitta fusca*)

SEASIDE STROLLS

One of the best ways of getting some fresh air and lifting your spirits, regardless of the time of year, is to take a coastal walk. Whether you want to take a gentle stroll along a vast sandy beach or stride across the cliffs while the waves crash beneath you, Britain's coastline has something for everyone.

Before you set off on a walk, make sure you are prepared. Wear suitable clothes and comfortable shoes with a good grip, as some of the paths can be slippery and steep. Some of these walks will take you across beaches, so check the tides in advance. Other

walks will take you along designated coastal paths, and you might find it helpful to take an Ordnance Survey map of the area with you.

Here is a selection of some of the most interesting and evocative walks around the British Isles.

❧ Calgary Bay, Isle of Mull, Scotland ❧

This is one of the most beautiful bays on the Isle of Mull, and when some of the islanders emigrated to a place in Alberta, Canada, they named it Calgary. You can see plenty of wildlife here.

❧ Holkham Bay, North Norfolk ❧

This is an easy walk that gives you spectacular views of the sea, as well as the chance to see many of the birds that flock to this part of the Norfolk coast.

❧ Holy Island, Northumberland ❧

Tread in the footsteps of pilgrims as you walk along the causeway to Holy Island, with its priory and Lindisfarne Castle. It's wise to check the crossing times of the causeway before you set out to avoid being cut off by the tide.

❧ Llŷn Peninsula, Wales ❧

You'll be spoilt for choice around this lovely stretch of coastline in North Wales, as it's fringed with sandy beaches. Suitable beaches include Porth Ceiriad. If you fancy a stiff climb, the path from Llanbedrog up to the top of Myndd Tir-y-cwmwd will give you fabulous views of the coastline.

❧ Seven Sisters, East Sussex ❧

These cliffs lie between Eastbourne and Cuckmere Haven, an old smuggler's haunt. If you start at Birling Gap, another smuggler's haven, you will have a brisk walk up and down the Seven Sisters, taking you past the red and white lighthouse at Beachy Head. This is part of the South Downs Way. The Seven Sisters are so-named because they consist of seven peaks; from west to east, they are Haven Brow, Short Brow, Rough Brow, Brass Point, Flat Hill, Bailey's Hill and Went Hill.

⇌ Solway Firth, Cumbria ⇌

Leave the crowds thronging the Lake District far behind you as you walk across this beautiful stretch of sand from the village of Cardurnock northwards towards Bowness-on-Solway.

⇌ Zennor to St Ives, Cornwall ⇌

If you crave spectacular scenery, this is the walk for you. Starting in Zennor, you take the South-West Coast Path to Porthmeor Beach at St Ives. If you're feeling energetic, you can continue along the coast path to Hayle, where you can have a paddle on Porth Kidney Sands before retracing your steps.

BEACHSIDE READING

Seaside settings have long been the inspiration for many writers, whether they wrote about the places themselves or used them as triggers for imaginary places. The number of British seaside towns and villages that have been mentioned in novels and poems, or which have been the homes of writers, would fill a book of their own, so here is a small selection.

Brighton, East Sussex

Rollicking, busy Brighton has a long list of literary credentials. It's cropped up in many novels over the years, including *Dombey and Son* (1848) by Charles Dickens; *Pride and Prejudice* (1813) by Jane Austen; *Vanity Fair* (1848) by William Thackeray; *Of Human Bondage* (1915) by W Somerset Maugham; and *Travels with my Aunt* (1969) by Graham Greene. It wasn't the first time Greene had written about Brighton. His novel, *Brighton Rock* (1938), is the book most closely associated with the town, and particularly with its seedier side.

Cornwall

This county deserves a special mention because the Cornish coast-line appears in so many novels and poems. Some writers are indissolubly linked with Cornwall, whether they wrote about real places or invented their own. Daphne du Maurier, who enjoyed many visits with her family in their holiday home at Fowey, made the county her home and set many of her most famous novels here. Those with coastal settings include *Rebecca* (1938) and *Frenchman's Creek* (1942). In more recent years, Mary Wesley chose Cornwall as the setting for several of her novels. In *The Camomile Lawn* (1984), which made her name, some of the younger characters race along 'the Terror Run' – a cliff-top path – at night.

Isle of Raasay, Highland

Sorley MacLean (Somhairle MacGill-Eain in Gaelic), who was born in Oskaig on Raasay in 1911, is recognised as one of the great Gaelic poets of the 20th century. Gaelic was his first language, and he only learnt English when he went to school in Portree on the Isle of Skye. He originally wrote poetry in English but from the 1930s began writing it only in Gaelic and destroyed all English versions of his poems. He worked as a teacher on Ross and the Isle of Mull before moving to Skye.

Laugharne, Carmarthenshire

Wales can boast of many writers and poets, but one of the most popular is Dylan Thomas, who spent several years in the fishing village of Laugharne. At first, he and his new bride Caitlin stayed with their friend Richard Hughes, who was the author of *A High Wind in Jamaica* (1929), but then they moved into their own home. After living in several different places they finally found The Boathouse (now open to the public). Although they were happy in Laugharne at first, their feelings for the town gradually changed. Thomas's most famous work, *Under Milk Wood* (1951), records 24 hours in the life of Llareggub (try spelling it backwards), which was a fictionalised version of Laugharne. He is buried in St Martin's churchyard.

Lyme Regis, Dorset

If you gathered together all the characters that have appeared in books set in Lyme Regis, there would barely be room for you to be there as well. One of the town's earliest appearances in print is in Jane Austen's *Persuasion* (first published in 1817), when Louisa Musgrove topples off the Cobb (the curved harbour wall). This scene made such an impression on the poet, Alfred, Lord Tennyson, that when he visited the town in 1867 he headed straight for the Cobb, saying, 'Show me the steps from which Louisa Musgrove fell!' In 1969 Lyme Regis again made it into print with the publication of *The French Lieutenant's Woman* by John Fowles. His heroine, Sarah Woodruff, spends a lot of time standing on the Cobb while looking out to sea. Lyme Regis also features in Tracy Chevalier's 2009 novel, *Remarkable Creatures*, which tells the true story of Mary Anning, the young woman who discovered all manner of important fossils along the Jurassic coastline in the early 19th century.

⇜ Whitby, North Yorkshire ⇝

Although Mrs Gaskell wrote about Whitby (disguised as Monkshaven) in her novel *Sylvia's Lovers* (1863), the town has a much stronger connection with a world-famous Victorian novel. This is *Dracula* (1897), in which the eponymous Count Dracula arrives in England from Transylvania and, you might say, really gets his teeth into the area. Bram Stoker was inspired to write the novel after sitting on the cliffs above Whitby Bay and watching a ship sail into the harbour.

THE CINQUE PORTS

Residents of the south-east corner of England always know if they're talking to a local or a visitor. It's the pronunciation of 'Cinque Ports' that gives the game away. Although you might expect them to be pronounced 'sank', in the French manner, the local pronunciation is 'sink'. And it gets still more complicated. Their French name implies that there are five of them (*cinque* is French for 'five'), but there are now 14. And the 'ports' part of their name is misleading, too, because some of the towns are now inland.

The Cinque Ports were formed before the Norman Conquest, during the reign of Edward the Confessor in the middle of the 11th century. There were five head ports – Dover, Hastings, Hythe, Romney and Sandwich – to which the 'antient towns' of Rye and Winchelsea were eventually added. Together, they carried out a range of duties known as ship service, which included providing a total of 57 ships, with a crew of 21 men, for 15 days each year. In return, they were all given freedom from various forms of taxation incurred at the ports.

Providing ship service was costly, despite the tax breaks, so the ports enlisted the help of small towns and villages, known as members or limbs. At one point there were 23 limbs, which stretched from Seaford in Sussex to Brightlingsea in Essex. Their most important function was to protect the vulnerable south-east coast against the ever-present threat of invasion: something they were unable to do in October 1066 when the French fleet arrived at Pevensey.

When the Royal Navy was established in the 17th century, the role of the Cinque Ports changed. They no longer had to provide ship service, so they lost some of their privileges. Nevertheless, the confederation of ports still exists, and the Cinque Ports Court of Admiralty has jurisdiction over a large area of the North Sea and the English Channel. The number of head ports remains the same, although New Romney has taken over from Romney. In addition, there are seven corporate members: Deal, Faversham, Folkestone, Lydd, Margate, Ramsgate and Tenterden.

Taken by the Sea

Britain's coastline is always changing. Some areas are growing as successive tides bring silt and shingle, while others are shrinking because the sea is gradually eroding them. And some towns and villages have been lost completely.

⫷ Dunwich, Suffolk ⫸

In Saxon times, the Suffolk town of Dunwich was a prosperous port and home to the first Bishop of East Anglia. Royal charters were bestowed on it for a mint and a market. By the time Domesday Book was compiled between 1085 and 1087, so William I could take a complete inventory of his newly conquered land and discover how much money it would provide through taxation, Dunwich had grown to become one of the ten largest towns in England. This was mostly as a result of its revenues from fishing and maritime trade. However, although the sea brought riches, it could also take them away. Already, in the time between William I's arrival in 1066 and the compilation of Domesday, over half the taxable farmland of Dunwich had been eroded and lost to the relentless sea. Major storms didn't help, with more land taken in 1328 and over 400 houses lost to the waves in 1347. Each century brought more problems as more of the town was eroded by the sea. In 1740 powerful storms demolished most of what was left, with only All Saints church still standing. It was only a matter of time before this too began to topple over the edge of the cliffs as the sea worked away at them, and now almost nothing is left of it. Nearby Greyfriars Monastery, which is the final relic of Dunwich's ecclesiastical history, is also starting to disappear into the sea.

❧ Hallsands, Devon ❧

When 650,000 tons of shingle were removed from the seabed and foreshore at the southernmost part of Start Bay in Devon, it was the beginning of the end for the small but successful fishing village of Hallsands. The Admiralty wanted to expand its docks at Devonport, and for this it needed masses of gravel and sand. Dredging began in the spring of 1897, much to the horror of the villagers and the inhabitants of neighbouring Beesands because they hadn't been consulted. By 1900, the level of the beach began to drop, and the damage was so great that dredging stopped in 1902. But it was too late. In 1903 part of the sea wall that had been built to protect Hallsands from the sea caved in. Although it was repaired, more depredations followed. Finally, the end came on 26 January 1917 when a terrible storm coincided with a very high tide. The waves threw tons of shingle at the houses, almost all of which collapsed. Nearly every inhabitant of Hallsands was now homeless and forced to move away, although a couple of people remained because their houses were left intact.

❧ Kenfig, Swansea ❧

Kenfig Sands lie just north of Porthcawl along Swansea Bay. Today you wouldn't know that they hide the town and borough of Kenfig, which was founded by Robert, Earl of Gloucester in about 1140. Although Kenfig was a thriving place, it was soon in jeopardy from the encroaching sand. The town was already surrounded by sand dunes but a combination of these, years in which the sea level rose and the tides were higher, and prevailing winds that blew the sand off the dunes towards Kenfig meant that the town became hidden beneath ever thicker layers of sand. Gradually, everyone moved away, leaving their town to the mercies of the sea and the sand. Today all that remains is a small amount of masonry which, ironically, belongs to the castle that once stood sentinel over the town.

⪻ Winchelsea, East Sussex ⪼

If you visit Winchelsea in East Sussex today, it looks delightfully old with its medieval buildings and bastide design. So it may come as a surprise to learn that it replaced Old Winchelsea, which was built on a long shingle bank that ran from nearby Fairlight to Hythe. A succession of violent storms in the 13th century, but especially the terrible storms of October 1250 and January 1252, broke up this shingle bank and the town was gradually buried beneath the incoming waves. In 1281 Edward I ordered that the town be rebuilt on the site where 'New' Winchelsea stands today.

DANGEROUS WATERS

Some stretches of the British coast are perilous. The sea may look calm when you're surveying it from the shore but it can hide treacherous rocks, submerged wrecks, sandbanks and powerful currents.

❧ The Bitches, Pembrokeshire ❧

You'll find this small but dangerous stretch of sea off Ramsey Island and the Welsh mainland. The sea is squeezed through the gap, where the dramatic differences in the level of the seabed, plus the shapes of the rocks, turn the water into a series of whirlpools.

Legends about the rocks revolve around the 6th-century saint Justinian who once lived on Ramsey Island. It's claimed that he used an axe to sever the strip of land that once linked the island to the mainland, and all that's left are the rocks collectively known as the Bitches.

❧ Goodwin Sands, Kent ❧

This long sandbar lies off Deal on the Kent coast, and it has such a powerful and ominous reputation that it's known as the 'Ship Swallower'. More than 1,000 shipwrecks have been recorded here over the centuries, although the real number of ruined vessels may be much higher. Bizarrely, the sands are strong enough to stand on at low tide, and cricket matches have even been held on them. But when the tide starts to come in, the Goodwin Sands are not the place to be because what was firm sand becomes so soft that it is easy to get sucked into it.

Naturally, legend surrounds this notorious stretch of sea. The sands are thought to be named after Earl Godwin, who was a powerful Anglo-Saxon landowner in the 11th century. There is a theory that the sands are all that's left of an island called Lomea, which Godwin owned and which was destroyed during a storm. However, drilling surveys of the sands show no evidence of this, and it's far more likely – although much less romantic – that they are an accumulation of sediment that's been washed through the narrow Strait of Dover over many centuries.

Gulf of Correyvreckan, Argyll and Bute

Corryvreckan has the distinction of being the third-largest whirlpool in the world, and it lies in the Inner Hebrides between the islands of Jura and Scarba. When conditions are right and there's a flood tide, you can hear its roar from ten miles (sixteen km) away. That might be the best place to be, as the waves can reach as high as thirty feet (nine metres). Not surprisingly, this tidal race has claimed the lives of many sailors and been responsible for many shipwrecks, as has the nearby Little Corryvreckan, which is also known as Grey Dogs.

In Scottish mythology, the whirlpool is the domain of Cailleach Bheur, who marks the turning of autumn to winter by washing her great plaid in its racing waters. When the tartan cloth finally emerges it's pure white and becomes the thick snow that lies across the islands.

Local legend states that in the 7th century this treacherous stretch of sea wrecked the entire fleet of 50 ships belonging to a man called Breccan. Later, one of Breccan's ribs surfaced from the waters to greet St Columba as he sailed past.

Gwennap Head, Cornwall

This piece of headland lies to the south of Land's End and looks out across the Atlantic towards the Isles of Scilly. It is one of the most treacherous stretches of sea off the British mainland. Not only do two major stretches of water meet here – St George's Channel and the English Channel – but the resulting tides are made even more hazardous by Wolf Rock and the Runnel Stone Reef which both lie nearby. Wolf Rock has claimed many lives but is now illuminated by its own lighthouse. Runnel Stone Reef, previously called the Rundle, lies between Hella Point and Gwennap Head. It's marked with a buoy and two day markers.

BEACONS IN THE DARK

The British coastline is full of navigational hazards, from rocks and cliffs to sandbanks. A chain of lighthouses runs around the coast, and each one has a unique way of identifying itself according to the colour and frequency of its light.

This list runs clockwise, starting with the northernmost lighthouse in the British Isles. Lighthouses in England and Wales are maintained and run by Trinity House, while those in Scotland and the Isle of Man are run by the Northern Lighthouse Board.

Muckle Flugga	60° 51'N, 00° 53'W
Uyea Sound	60° 41'N, 00° 55'W
Whitehill	60° 35'N, 01° 00'W
Out Skerries Lighthouse	60° 25'N, 00° 44'W
Wether Holm	60° 22'N, 01° 01'W
Bressay Lighthouse	60° 07'N, 01° 07'W
Sumburgh Head	59° 51'N, 01° 16'W
Fair Isle North	59° 33'N, 01° 36'W
Fair Isle South	59° 31'N, 01° 39'W
North Ronaldsay	59° 23'N, 02° 23'W

Start Point . . . . 59° 17'N, 02° 23'W
Auskerry . . . . 59° 02'N, 02° 34'W
Copinsay . . . . 58° 54'N, 02° 40'W
Pentland Skerries . . . . 58° 41'N, 02° 55'W
Duncansby Head . . . . 58° 37'N, 03° 01'W
Noss Head . . . . 58° 29'N, 03° 03'W
Tarbat Ness . . . . 57° 52'N, 03° 47'W
Cromarty . . . . 57° 41'N, 04° 02'W
Chanonry . . . . 57° 34'N, 04° 05'W
Covesea . . . . 57° 43'N, 03° 20'W
Kinnaird Head . . . . 57° 41'N, 02° 00'W
Rattray Head . . . . 57° 37'N, 01° 49'W
Buchan Ness . . . . 57° 28'N, 01° 46'W
Girdle Ness . . . . 57° 08'N, 02° 03'W
Tod Head . . . . 56° 53'N, 02° 13'W
Scudie Ness . . . . 56° 42'N, 02° 26'W
Bell Rock . . . . 56° 26'N, 02° 23'W
Fife Ness . . . . 56° 17'N, 02° 35'W
Isle of May . . . . 56° 11'N, 02° 33'W
Inchkeith . . . . 56° 02'N, 03° 08'W
Fidra . . . . 56° 04'N, 02° 47'W
Bass Rock . . . . 56° 05'N, 02° 38'W
Barns Ness . . . . 55° 59'N, 02° 27'W
St Abbs Head . . . . 55° 55'N, 02° 08'W
Heugh Hill Lighthouse . . . . 55° 40'N, 01° 48'W
Guile Point East Lighthouse . . . . 55° 39'N, 01° 47'W
Longstone Lighthouse . . . . 55° 39'N, 01° 37'W
Bamburgh Lighthouse . . . . 55° 37'N, 01° 43'W
Farne Lighthouse . . . . 55° 37'N, 01° 39'W
Coquet Lighthouse . . . . 55° 20'N, 01° 32'W
Whitby Lighthouse . . . . 54° 29'N, 00° 34'W
Flamborough Lighthouse . . . . 54° 07'N, 00° 05'W
Cromer Lighthouse . . . . 52° 55'N, 01° 19'E
Lowestoft Lighthouse . . . . 52° 29'N, 01° 45'E

Southwold Lighthouse . . . . 52° 20'N, 01° 41'E
Orfordness Lighthouse. . . . . 52° 05'N, 01° 35'E
North Foreland Lighthouse . . . . 51° 22'N, 01° 27'E
Dungeness Lighthouse. . . . . 50° 55'N, 00° 59'E
Royal Sovereign . . . . 50° 43'N, 00° 26'E
Beachy Head . . . . 50° 44'N, 00° 14'E
Nab Tower Lighthouse. . . . . 50° 40'N, 00° 57'W
St Catherine's Lighthouse . . . . 50° 34'N, 01° 18'W
Needles Lighthouse . . . . 50° 40'N, 01° 35'W
Anvil Point Lighthouse. . . . . 50° 35'N, 01° 57'W
Portland Bill Lighthouse . . . . 50° 31'N, 02° 27'W
Casquets Lighthouse . . . . 49° 43'N, 02° 23'W
Alderney Lighthouse . . . . 49° 44'N, 02° 10'W
Les Hanois Lighthouse . . . . 49° 26'N, 02° 42'W
Sark Lighthouse . . . . 49° 26'N, 02° 21'W
Berry Head Lighthouse . . . . 50° 24'N, 03° 29'W
Start Point Lighthouse . . . . 50° 13'N, 03° 38'W
Eddystone Lighthouse . . . . 50° 11'N, 04° 16'W
St Anthony's Lighthouse . . . . 50° 08'N, 05° 01'W
Lizard Lighthouse . . . . 49° 58'N, 05° 12'W
Tater Du Lighthouse . . . . 50° 03'N, 05° 35'W
Wolf Rock Lighthouse . . . . 49° 57'N, 05° 48'W
Penninis Lighthouse. . . . . 49° 54'N, 06° 18'W
Round Island Lighthouse . . . . 49° 59'N, 06° 19'W
Bishop Rock Lighthouse . . . . 49° 52'N, 06° 27'W
Longships Lighthouse . . . . 50° 04'N, 05° 45'W
Pendeen Lighthouse. . . . . 50° 10'N, 05° 40'W
Godrevy Lighthouse. . . . . 50° 14'N, 05° 24'W
Trevose Head Lighthouse . . . . 50° 33'N, 05° 03'W
Hartland Point Lighthouse . . . . 51° 01'N, 04° 31'W
Crow Point Lighthouse . . . . 51° 04'N, 04° 11'W
Lundy North Lighthouse . . . . 51° 12'N, 04° 41'W
Lundy South Lighthouse . . . . 51° 09'N, 04° 39'W
Bull Point Lighthouse . . . . 51° 12'N, 04° 12'W

Lynmouth Foreland Lighthouse .... 51° 15'N, 03° 47'W
Flatholm Lighthouse .... 51° 22'N, 03° 07'W
Monkstone Lighthouse .... 51° 25'N, 03° 06'W
Blacknore Point Lighthouse........... 51° 29'N, 02° 48'W
Nash Point Lighthouse .... 51° 24'N, 03° 33'W
Mumbles Lighthouse .... 51° 34'N, 03° 58'W
Caldey Island Lighthouse.............. 51° 38'N, 04° 41'W
St Anne's Head Lighthouse .... 51° 41'N, 05° 10'W
Skokholm Lighthouse................. 51° 42'N, 05° 17'W
Smalls Lighthouse .... 51° 43'N, 05° 40'W
South Bishop Lighthouse.............. 51° 51'N, 05° 25'W
Strumble Head Lighthouse .... 52° 02'N, 05° 04'W
St Tudwal's Lighthouse .... 52° 48'N, 04° 28'W
Bardsey Lighthouse .... 52° 45'N, 04° 48'W
South Stack Lighthouse .... 53° 18'N, 04° 42'W
The Skerries Lighthouse............... 53° 25'N, 04° 36'W
Point Lynas Lighthouse .... 53° 25'N, 04° 17'W
Trywyn Du Lighthouse................ 53° 19'N, 04° 02'W
Hilbre Island Lighthouse .... 53° 23'N, 03° 14'W
Chicken Rock....................... 54° 02'N, 04° 50'W
Calf of Man .... 54° 03'N, 04° 50'W
Thousla Rock .... 54° 04'N, 04° 48'W
Langness........................... 54° 03'N, 04° 38'W
Douglas Head .... 54° 08'N, 04° 28'W
Maughold Head..................... 54° 18'N, 04° 18'W
Point of Ayre .... 54° 29'N, 04° 22'W
The Winkie Lighthouse .... 54° 25'N, 04° 22'W
St Bees Lighthouse.................. 54° 31'N, 03° 38'W
Maryport Lighthouse................. 54° 43'N, 03° 30'W
Mull of Galloway .... 54° 38'N, 04° 51'W
Killantringan....................... 54° 52'N, 05° 09'W
Corsewall .... 55° 00'N, 05° 09'W
Ailsa Craig .... 55° 15'N, 05° 06'W
Turnberry .... 55° 19'N, 04° 51'W

Pladda. . . . . 55° 25'N, 05° 07'W
Davaar . . . . 55° 26'N, 05° 32'W
Sanda . . . . 55° 16'N, 05° 35'W
Mull of Kintyre. . . . . 55° 19'N, 05° 48'W
Rinns of Islay . . . . 55° 40'N, 06° 31'W
Ruvaal. . . . . 55° 56'N, 06° 07'W
Dubh Artach . . . . 56° 08'N, 06° 38'W
Skerryvore. . . . . 56° 19'N, 07° 07'W
Lismore . . . . 56° 27'N, 05° 36 W
Ardtornish . . . . 56° 31'N, 05° 45'W
Ardmore. . . . . 56° 39'N, 06° 08'W
Ardnamurchan . . . . 56° 44'N, 06° 13'W
Hyskeir. . . . . 56° 58'N, 06° 41'W
Barra Head. . . . . 56° 47'N, 07° 39'W
Ornsay . . . . 57° 09'N, 05° 47'W
Ardtreck . . . . 57° 20'N, 06° 26'W
Neist Point. . . . . 57° 25'N, 06° 47'W
Ushenish . . . . 57° 18'N, 07° 11'W
Monach . . . . 57° 31'N, 07° 42'W
Weavers Point . . . . 57° 36'N, 07° 06'W
Vaternish . . . . 57° 36'N, 06° 38'W
An T-lasgair . . . . 57° 41'N, 06° 26'W

Rona . . . . 57° 35'N, 05° 57'W
Rubh Re . . . . 57° 51'N, 05° 49'W
Eilean Glas . . . . 57° 51'N, 06° 38'W
Flannan Islands . . . . 58° 17'N, 07° 35'W
Butt of Lewis . . . . 58° 31'N, 06° 16'W
Tiumpan Head . . . . 58° 16'N, 06° 08'W
Stoer Head . . . . 58° 14'N, 05° 24'W
Cape Wrath . . . . 58° 37'N, 05° 00'W
Sule Skerry . . . . 59° 05'N, 04° 24'W
Strathy Point . . . . 58° 36'N, 04° 01'W
Holburn Head . . . . 58° 37'N, 03° 32'W
Dunnet Head . . . . 58° 40'N, 03° 22'W
Stroma . . . . 58° 42'N, 03° 07'W
Cantick Head . . . . 58° 47'N, 03° 08'W
Tor Ness . . . . 58° 47'N, 03° 17'W
Barrel of Butter . . . . 58° 53'N, 03° 07'W
Brough of Birsay . . . . 59° 08'N, 03° 20'W
Noup Head . . . . 59° 20'N, 03° 04'W
Foula . . . . 60° 07'N, 02° 04'W
Bullia Skerry . . . . 60° 07'N, 01° 21'W
Valia Sound . . . . 60° 12'N, 01° 33'W
Ve Skerries . . . . 60° 22'N, 01° 49'W
Eshaness . . . . 60° 29'N, 01° 38'W
Bagi Stack . . . . 60° 43'N, 01° 07'W

Coastal Curiosities

The intricate British coastline stretches for thousands of miles, giving us everything from tranquil stretches of white sand to rugged coasts where black rocks rise up out of the sea like jagged teeth. Every area of the coastline has its own charm, but some are particularly interesting.

Chesil Beach, Dorset

Once seen, never forgotten. Chesil Beach is a narrow pebble beach that stretches for 18 miles (30 km) between Portland and West Bay. Its correct geological name is a 'tombolo' – a strip of shingle or sand that joins an island (in this case, the Isle of Portland) to the mainland. It encloses a salt lagoon called the Fleet and is an extraordinary sight, but one of its most astonishing features is that the pebbles on it are graded in size, as though a giant has been playing with them and neatly arranging them in order. The biggest pebbles are at the Portland end, with the tiniest at Bridport. How did Chesil Beach get there and how does the sea sift the pebbles so precisely? No one is quite sure, so maybe a giant is at work after all.

Durdle Door, Dorset

This rock formation looks like a seahorse – or possibly even the Loch Ness Monster dipping its head into the sea. It's an arch that has been created by the sea gradually eroding the softer rocks until only the hard limestones are left. It gets its name from the Old English word *thirl*, which means 'to drill'. It is one of the many spectacular features of what is known as the Jurassic Coast – England's first natural World Heritage Site that encompasses the Dorset and East Devon coastlines. It's called the Jurassic Coast because some parts of it were formed during the Jurassic geological period, between 145 and 200 million years ago, when a tropical sea flooded the desert that had been here. Generally speaking, the oldest rocks are in the west of the Jurassic Coast and progressively younger ones are in the east.

Old Man of Hoy, Orkney Islands

This red sandstone sea stack towers 449 feet (137 metres) high near Rackwick Bay on the island of Hoy. It is believed to be about 400 years old, and probably got its name because it originally had an arch at its base that looked like a pair of legs. One of the legs has long gone, and it's thought that the rest of the Old Man will eventually be eroded by the sea and wind until nothing is left of it.

❧ Spurn Head, East Yorkshire ❧

Spurn Head is a spit of sand and shingle that curls like a long finger around the north-eastern point of the Humber Estuary. It's made of material that is eroded from the Holderness coastline and washed down from Flamborough Head in the north. Once it reaches Spurn Head, the material is held in place by the marram grass that grows here.

❧ White Cliffs of Dover, Kent ❧

These chalk cliffs, flecked with black flints, have an iconic place in many British hearts. Straddling the coastline either side of Dover, these cliffs look out across the Strait of Dover to France and appear to be protecting Britain from invaders. In the days before air travel, most people sailed to mainland Europe from Dover. The cliffs were their last view of Britain when they left and the first when they returned. They were a particularly stirring patriotic symbol during the Second World War.

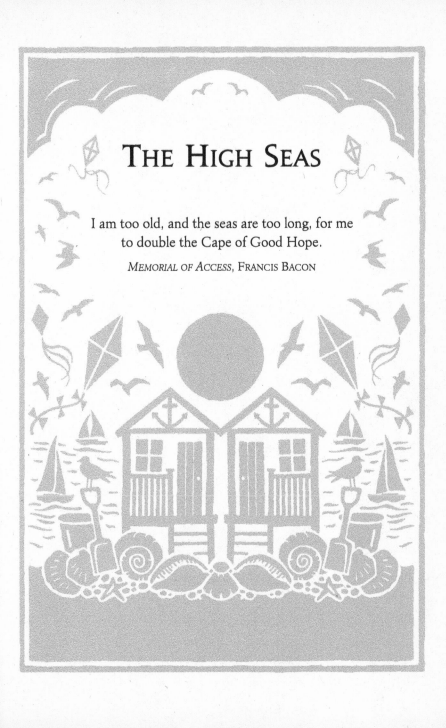

THE HIGH SEAS

I am too old, and the seas are too long, for me
to double the Cape of Good Hope.

MEMORIAL OF ACCESS, FRANCIS BACON

CROSSING THE ENGLISH CHANNEL

The French know it as *la Manche*, or 'the sleeve'. But from the 18th century onwards, the British have laid claim to this stretch of water by calling it the English Channel. This is the narrow strip of sea that separates southern England from northern France. It marks the point where the Atlantic Ocean, to Britain's west, meets the North Sea to Britain's east. It's a relatively modest area of sea in many ways, being the smallest of all the shallow seas around Europe, yet it's one of the busiest shipping lanes in the world and carries over 400 ships a day. You have only to stand on a beach overlooking the English Channel to see that: there is usually the silhouette of at least one gigantic container ship on the horizon, not to mention cross-Channel ferries and plenty of smaller craft.

Not surprisingly, there are bound to be accidents with so many ships passing through these waters every day. Things had got so bad by early 1971 that the world's first radar-controlled Traffic Separation System was set up by the International Maritime Organization to try to control the situation. This was called the Dover Traffic Separation System and it has dramatically helped to reduce the number of collisions that take place each year. The main British ferry ports for the English Channel are Dover, Newhaven, Portsmouth, Poole, Weymouth and Plymouth.

❧ Swim for it! ❧

It isn't only ships that cross from one side of the Channel to the other: plenty of swimmers have done it too. Quite sensibly, they always choose the narrowest section of the Channel, which is the Strait of Dover – a mere 21 miles (34 km), which doubtless looks quite achievable on a map but is a daunting prospect in reality.

 The first person to attempt this maritime feat, unassisted and observed, was Captain Matthew Webb, who swam from Dover to Calais from 24 to 25 August 1875. It took him 21 hours and 45 minutes. By 1927, all sorts of people were claiming to have matched Webb's endurance test even though most of them couldn't prove it, so the Channel Swimming Association (CSA) was set up to monitor and officiate these attempted crossings. In 1999 the CSA was superseded by two new bodies: the CSA (Ltd) and the Channel Swimming and Piloting Federation.

The swimming times have vastly improved since Webb's day. To date, the record is held by Petar Stoychev, a Bulgarian open water swimmer who crossed the Channel in 6 hours and 57 minutes on 25 August 2007. The date of his triumph was the anniversary of Webb's achievement.

If you're contemplating swimming the Channel, August is the best month to do it, and statistically 28 August is the best day of all, as so far there have been 47 successful swims on that date.

❧ Going by air ❧

Since January 1785, when the first unusual cross-Channel journey was successfully accomplished by Jean-Pierre Blanchard and John Jeffries in a helium balloon, people have thought of all sorts of headline-catching methods for getting across the Channel. But on 23 August 1910, the first aircraft made the crossing. It was piloted by the American aviator John Bevins Moisant. He took two passengers: his mechanic, Albert Fileux, and his cat, the wonderfully named Mademoiselle Fifi.

BRITISH WATERS

How many major stretches of water are there around the British coastline? There may be more than you imagine. This list, which includes massive bays, begins in the north-east of Scotland and works its way in as clockwise a direction as possible round Britain.

North Sea
Pentland Firth
Dornoch Firth
Cromarty Firth
Moray Firth
Firth of Tay
St Andrew's Bay
Firth of Forth
Mouth of the Humber
The Wash
Strait of Dover
English Channel
Spithead
The Solent
Southampton Water
Poole Bay
Lyme Bay
Babbacombe Bay
Tor Bay
Start Bay
Bigbury Bay
Whitsand Bay
St Austell Bay
Carrick Roads
Falmouth Bay

Mounts Bay
St George's Channel
Celtic Sea
Bude Bay
Barnstaple, or Bideford, Bay
Bristol Channel
Bridgwater Bay
Mouth of the Severn
Swansea Bay
Carmarthen Bay
Milford Haven
Broad Sound
St Brides Bay
Cardigan Bay (Bae Ceredigion)
Irish Sea
Tremadog Bay
Bardsey Sound (Swint Enlli)
Caernarfon Bay
Menai Strait (Afon Menai)
Holyhead Bay
Conwy Bay
Liverpool Bay
Morecambe Bay
Lancaster Sound
Solway Firth
Wigtown Bay
Luce Bay
Ramsey Bay
Firth of Clyde
North Channel, or Straits of Moyle
Sound of Bute
Kilbrannan Sound
Belfast Lough
Loch Fyne

Sound of Jura
Firth of Clyde
Sound of Bute
Firth of Lorn
Sound of Iona
Loch Scridain
Loch na Keeal
Loch Tuath
Sound of Mull
Loch Linnhe
Loch Sunart
Sound of Arisaig
Loch Nevis
Loch Hourn
Loch Duich
Loch Alsh
Sound of Sleat
Sound of Rum
Sea of the Hebrides
Loch Carron
Loch Torridon
Inner Sound
Sound of Raasay
Loch Snizort
The Little Minch
Sea of the Hebrides
Sound of Barra (An Caolas Barrach)
Sound of Monach (Caolas Mhonach)
Sound of Harris
Sound of Shiant (Caolas Nan Eilean)
The Minch
Loch Gairloch
Loch Ewe
Gruinard Bay

Little Loch Broom
Loch Broom
Enard Bay
Eddrachillis Bay
Kyle of Tongue
Pentland Firth
Scapa Flow
Stronsay Firth
Westray Firth
The North Sound
North Ronaldsay Firth
Sumburgh Roost
St Magnus Bay
Yell Sound
Colgrave Sound
Sinclair's Bay
Spey Bay

WATERY NAMES

The British coastline abounds with interesting place names, as well as descriptive names for headlands and stretches of water. But what do they actually mean?

BAY This is an area of coastline where the sea is contained within an inward bend of the shoreline and where the opening is wide. The

British coastline is notched with bays, some of which are tiny and some of which are massive, such as Morecambe Bay.

FIRTH This describes an arm of the sea or a river estuary. It comes from the Old Norse word *fiord*. There are many firths in Scotland, which is where the word originated in Britain, including the Firth of Forth.

HAVEN This is an inlet of the sea or the mouth of a river that offers safety to ships and is a good place to weigh anchor, such as Milford Haven in Pembrokeshire.

HEAD As its name suggests, this describes an area of the coastline that projects into the sea, especially if it is much higher than its surroundings. The British coastline is full of such places, including Gribbin Head and Pencarrow Head in Cornwall.

KYLE This is the Gaelic word for a narrow channel of water, which is also known as a sound or a strait. The coastline of Western Scotland abounds in such places, including the Kyle of Lochalsh in Highland.

LOCH Although this Gaelic word is commonly given to a lake, it also describes an arm of the sea, particularly if it is narrow or partly land-locked: two good examples are Loch Snizort off the Isle of Skye, and Loch Fyne on the west coast of Argyll and Bute, which is the longest sea loch in Scotland.

NESS Many areas of coastline are called 'ness'. Orford Ness in Suffolk, for instance, is a long, narrow strip of land that extends several miles down the coastline. 'Ness' is another word for a headland, taken from the Middle Low German word *nes*. The Middle Dutch *nes* described land outside the dykes, and if you look at Orford Ness on a map you will see how beautifully that description fits.

POINT This is the tip of a stretch of land that runs out to sea, such as Hartland Point and Baggy Point in Devon.

ROADS How can you have roads in the sea? The word suggests a busy place with lots of shipping, whereas in this context it means a sheltered stretch of water near the shore, where ships can safely anchor. The Isle of Wight boasts both Cowes Roads and Ryde Roads.

SOUND This is a narrow channel of water, especially if it connects two large bodies of water or it lies between the mainland and an island. The Sound of Mull sits between the rugged coastline of mainland Scotland and the Isle of Mull.

SPIT This is a narrow tongue of land that projects from the shore into the surrounding sea. Spithead is a stretch of water off Portsmouth that got its name from a vast sandbank called the Spit that extends into the Solent from the coast.

STRAIT Often used in the plural, this is a narrow channel of water that connects two larger bodies of water. The Strait of Dover lies off the Kent coast.

GREAT SHIPS

Not every ship that has sailed into the history books belonged to the Navy. Some of them were privately owned. Here is a small selection of some of the ships that weren't owned by the Navy but which we still remember, sometimes centuries after they played their part in the rich and varied history of the British Isles.

✎ Golden Hind ✎

You can see two versions of this famous ship – a reconstruction of her in Brixham, Devon, and a replica that is as accurate as possible (named *The Golden Hinde*) in London. Their namesake was the ship most closely associated with Francis Drake when he circumnavigated the world in a voyage that lasted from 1577 to 1580. He set off from Plymouth in December 1577 with a fleet of five ships and fewer than 200 men in what was effectively a privateering operation licensed by Elizabeth I with specific instructions to wreak havoc on the Spanish. She told him she 'would gladly be revenged on the king of Spain for divers injuries that I have received'. Her word was his command...

Drake's flagship was originally called the *Pelican*, but he renamed her *Golden Hind* when he passed through the Strait of Magellan (discovered by Ferdinand Magellan in 1520) in August 1578. The voyage was a magnificent success because it bloodied the Spanish noses (which helped to trigger the Spanish Armada of 1588) and brought back treasure beyond compare, all of which had been plundered en route. Drake was knighted after sailing the *Golden Hind* back into Plymouth Harbour on 26 September 1580. He had lost many members of his crew but those that survived were allowed to share in the bounty.

Elizabeth was so delighted with Drake and his ship that she had the *Golden Hind* put in permanent dock in Deptford where it could be visited by a jubilant public. Sadly, the ship eventually rotted away in the late 17th century.

Incidentally, Drake became such a national hero that after he died he was commonly believed to be waiting in Heaven for the summons to come to his country's aid again – just like that other great hero, King Arthur.

❧ Mayflower ❧

On 16 September 1620 a privately owned ship called the *Mayflower* set sail from Plymouth with 102 passengers and a crew of about 30, under the captainship of Christopher Jones. They were embarking upon a huge adventure that would change the course of history, because these passengers were English Separatists who planned to set up a new religious colony in the far-off new land of America. They were Protestant Nonconformists who wanted to preserve their religious freedom from what they saw as the confines of the Church of England. Unfortunately, they had to endure several trials before they achieved their ambition.

The plan was for a group of the Pilgrims, as they became known, to sail from their home in the Netherlands to Southampton in their ship the *Speedwell*, collect a group of English Pilgrims, and then for them all to sail across the Atlantic in both the *Speedwell* and the *Mayflower* to the mouth of the Hudson River in what was then England's colony in Virginia. But things didn't turn out quite the way they'd intended. Everything began well, and both ships left Southampton on 15 August 1620, but the *Speedwell* started to take on water and had to be refitted at Dartmouth. Off they went again and got past Land's End, only to have to return to Plymouth this time because once again the *Speedwell* was leaking.

The only option was to leave her behind, and most of the passengers were squeezed on to the *Mayflower*, where they had to endure very cramped conditions, although a few decided to return to the Netherlands. It's not certain what happened next to the *Speedwell*, although it is now known that the crew had sabotaged her in order to escape being tied into their year-long contracts.

The *Mayflower* successfully set sail but encountered rough seas and storms on her journey across the North Atlantic. The plan to land in Virginia had to be changed, and on 21 November 1620 the ship made landfall at Cape Cod, in what is now Provincetown Harbour. Unfortunately, the Pilgrims had arrived at the start of a typically bitter New England winter, and onboard the *Mayflower* food was running short while tempers were running high. After some difficult encounters between the Pilgrims and the indigenous population, the ship sailed down to Plymouth in what is now Massachusetts, where the Pilgrims once more stayed onboard. Perhaps they should have taken their chances with the weather, because over half the passengers and crew died from several contagious diseases that spread like wildfire in those cramped conditions. When spring finally arrived, the surviving passengers built huts ashore and disembarked. Although they didn't know it at the time, they would be forever associated with their new land, which eventually became known as the United States of America.

The *Mayflower* began her voyage back to England on 5 April 1621 and arrived on 16 May. It's believed that she was dismantled for lumber at Rotherhithe in London in 1623. Another ship, also called the *Mayflower*, carried several groups of settlers across the Atlantic during four successful voyages, but sank during her fifth crossing in 1641.

ᦗ Gipsy Moth IV ᦗ

Both the *Golden Hind* and the *Mayflower* were large ships with a full crew, but *Gipsy Moth IV* was a 53-foot (16-metre) ketch-rigged sailing yacht that circumnavigated the world with only one man onboard. Francis Chichester had already achieved great things in the air, having made the first east–west flight across the Tasman Sea from New Zealand to Australia in 1931. He discovered the joys of sailing in the 1950s and won the first solo transatlantic race in 1960 when he took 40 days to sail *Gipsy Moth III* from Plymouth to New York City.

But even better things were to come. On 27 August 1966 Francis Chichester set out from Plymouth on *Gipsy Moth IV*, determined to beat the average time of 230 days in which Australian clipper ships once circumnavigated the globe. His intention was to reach Sydney, Australia, in 100 days, spend a month there and sail back to Britain in another 100 days. After encountering various problems with *Gipsy Moth IV*, Chichester sailed into Sydney on 12 December, having taken 107 days to get there. He set off for home again, via Cape Horn, on 29 January 1967 and sailed into Plymouth to a hero's welcome on 28 May. Although he had been away for 274 days, his sailing time was 226 days, which meant he'd achieved his ambition to beat the time of the old clippers. He broke several records, including that of completing the longest passage by a small sailing vessel without making any ports of call. Quite fittingly, he was knighted at the quayside by Queen Elizabeth II, who used the same sword that had knighted Sir Francis Drake in 1580.

Although Chichester died in 1972, it wasn't the end of *Gipsy Moth IV*'s career. After spending many years in dry dock next to the *Cutty Sark* in Greenwich, she took part in the Blue Water Round the World Rally in 2005, once again setting out from Plymouth, and after an eventful trip she sailed back home, docking at West Hoe Pier on 28 May 2007, exactly 40 years to the day after she had arrived in triumph. At the time, she was owned by the UK charity, UKSA (United Kingdom Sailing Academy), but in November 2010 she was sold to new British owners who will keep her at Cowes on the Isle of Wight.

JOHN HARRISON AND THE QUESTION OF LONGITUDE

How do you know exactly where you are when you're out at sea? Today this question is easily solved because we have many navigational aids at our disposal. But in the 17th century it was a knotty problem.

Although the Earth had been divided like an orange into longitudinal segments, running from the North to South poles, no one had any way of determining which area of longitude they occupied when out at sea. They didn't know how far east or west they were, which meant they didn't know if they were in danger of running aground, being wrecked on treacherous rocks or about to sail into a whirlpool. It also meant that if an exploratory voyage discovered a new land, the sailors had no means of finding it again. Latitude, which gives the position north or south of the Equator, was easily calculated using the angle of the sun over the horizon at noon, but longitude was a different matter because it related to the movement of the Earth, which couldn't be observed in the same way.

This seemingly intractable difficulty was tragically highlighted in many maritime disasters. Perhaps the greatest of these took place on 22 October 1707, when HMS *Association*, the flagship of Sir Cloudesley Shovell, plus the two other ships sailing with him, was wrecked on the Bishop and Clerk Rocks off the Isles of Scilly. The loss of three ships and almost 2,000 men – there was only one survivor and it wasn't Shovell – was due to errors that arose from the navigators being unable to calculate the longitude of their location. Something had to be done, and in 1714 Parliament set up a Board of Longitude to solve the problem. It offered the magnificent prize of £20,000 to the person who found a way of measuring longitude to an accuracy of 30 miles (48 km) after a six-week voyage to the West Indies.

The challenge greatly appealed to a Yorkshire horologist and inventor called John Harrison. He was convinced that the answer lay in devising a mechanical instrument that would be set to the time at Greenwich (the site of the Prime Meridian, which is the line of longitude that divides west and east), and would be able to compare that with the local time at any place on the globe. This put him at odds with the then Astronomer Royal, Nevil Maskelyne, who believed that the answer lay in tables that charted the positions of the moon and stars.

John Harrison devoted many years to the task of creating what became a chronometer. His first attempt, H1, was completed in 1735. It was cumbersome, weighing 72 pounds (32.6 kg), but accurate, and Harrison was awarded £500 for creating a minor discovery. He refined his design and his third attempt, H3, won him the Copley Medal from the Royal Society.

His fourth attempt, H4, was a pocket watch. He completed it in 1759 and it was tested on a voyage to Jamaica in 1761, when it was found to be accurate to 18 geographical miles (29 km), or one minute and 54 seconds. Success! But Maskelyne thought differently and persuaded the Board of Longitude not to award the prize to Harrison. H4 was tested again in 1764 on a voyage to Barbados and this time was found to be accurate within 10 miles (16 km). Even better! But still the Board refused to cough up.

An Act of Parliament ruled that Harrison would receive half the prize money if he could explain how the chronometer worked and if copies of it could be made by other craftsmen. Reluctantly, Harrison agreed to these new rules and a precise copy of H4, made by the watchmaker Larcum Kendall and known as K1, accompanied Captain James Cook on his second voyage to the southern hemisphere between 1772 and 1775. Cook was thrilled with the accuracy of the chronometer and made his feelings plain.

In the meantime, Harrison's son, William, intervened by appealing to George III, who was known for his keen interest in science. As a result of this, a now very bitter and disillusioned Harrison finally received over £8,000, but the Board insisted he wasn't being given the prize money, simply a bounty. A new Act of Parliament in 1773 moved the goalposts yet again by setting out much stricter criteria for the winning entry, so Harrison, who died in 1776, was never able to claim his prize. The 1773 Longitude Act wasn't repealed until 1828, when the prevaricating Board of Longitude was finally disbanded. If Charles Dickens had been writing about them he might have been tempted to call them the Circumlocution Board, which was the name he gave to the incompetent government department in his novel *Little Dorrit*.

A second copy of H4 is known as K2. It went on the mutinous voyage of HMS *Bounty* and is now in safekeeping at the National Maritime Museum in Greenwich.

THE MERCHANT NAVY

Unlike the Royal Navy, the Merchant Navy is not a single entity. It is the collective term for all the commercial shipping that is registered in the United Kingdom, and it's regulated by the Maritime and Coastguard Agency. Britain's merchant ships fly the Red Ensign, which is a red flag with the Union Flag in the top left quarter.

The first attempts to organise a merchant navy were made in the 17th century, so the Navy could draw on the services of accomplished seamen in times of national crisis. However, at first it wasn't a success and only properly got underway in 1835. The growth and expansion of the British Empire across the globe in the Victorian age made the British Merchant Service, as it was then known, the greatest in the world.

Merchant ships played a vital role in both the First and Second World Wars as they transported food, fuel, clothes and other necessities across the seas. They were particularly vulnerable to German U-boats, which seemed able to pick them off at will, causing great shortages of essentials in Britain. Many merchant sailors died in these attacks: over 14,000 died in the First World War and 30,000 in the Second World War. Such was the sacrifice in the First World War that George V, who had a naval background, renamed the service the Merchant Navy. The Prince of Wales (later Edward VIII) was made Master of the Merchant Navy.

The terrible loss of life sustained by the Merchant Navy during both wars, and the invaluable service its sailors performed while working in the extremely dangerous Atlantic convoys, entitles its members to lay wreaths of remembrance each Remembrance Day. Merchant sailors are eligible to receive the George Cross, which is the UK's highest civilian and military decoration for gallantry in action that is not in the face of the enemy. They can also receive the Distinguished Service Cross, which is awarded for gallantry at sea during active operations with the enemy.

WHO WAS THE REAL ROBINSON CRUSOE?

It's one of the most famous seafaring adventures ever written. Daniel Defoe's novel *Robinson Crusoe* was first published in 1719. It recounted the 'strange surprising adventures' of a man who for 28 years was a castaway on an uninhabited island off the coast of America. He freed a prisoner from some visiting cannibals and called him Friday, as that was the day of the week when they met. They eventually got off the island and, such was the success of the book, they went on to have more escapades in a sequel called *The Farther Adventures of Robinson Crusoe*.

Defoe was a journalist and it's always been believed that he modelled Robinson Crusoe on a real-life castaway. We will probably never be completely certain about this man's identity, but for many years it's been thought that he was Alexander Selkirk. He set sail in 1703 as a privateer (a sailor or ship that carried a letter of commission, which gave it an official seal of approval for the capture of cargoes or ships belonging to other countries) in a convoy of two ships. After falling out with the first lieutenant of his ship, the *Cinque Ports*, Selkirk asked to be left behind on the Juan Fernandez Islands. As soon as the *Cinque Ports* prepared to set sail, Selkirk had second thoughts but it was too late and the ship sailed without him. Perhaps it was just as well, because she sank soon afterwards and the few survivors were captured by the Spanish. Selkirk spent the next four and a half years on his island, with only goats for company, until the *Duke*, an English privateer, dropped anchor on the island. The crew were astonished to see Selkirk, who was almost delirious with joy at being rescued but had forgotten how to speak. Selkirk returned to England with the ship, amid much celebration.

However, there is another contender for the honour of being the original Robinson Crusoe, and it's thought that Defoe met him because they shared the same publisher. Henry Pitman was an English surgeon who was convicted of taking part in the Duke of Monmouth's rebellion (a failed attempt to overthrow James II in 1685). His punishment was to be transported as a convict to Barbados for ten years. He and some fellow convicts escaped in 1687, eventually making landfall on the island of Salt Tortuga, off the Venezuelan coast. Pitman and his fellow crewmen were marooned on the island by a Spanish pirate, from whom Pitman had bought an Indian prisoner (cue Man Friday). The idea was that he would help them all to survive. Three months later, another pirate ship arrived and was glad to welcome Pitman onboard – surgical skills were always in great demand. Pitman is said to have left the other sailors on the island, so perhaps they were considered surplus to requirements. After he had safely returned to London, in 1689 he wrote a book about his adventures, with the snappy title of *A Relation of the Great Sufferings and Strange Adventures of Henry Pitman, Chirugeon to the Late Duke of Monmouth*. An added bonus of getting back on dry land must have been that James II had legged it by then, having abdicated the throne in favour of his daughter and son-in-law.

UNWELCOME VISITORS

We are waiting for the long-promised invasion.
So are the fishes.

WINSTON CHURCHILL, 21 OCTOBER 1941

Rule Britannia!

Back in the days of Julius Caesar, the Romans knew the British Isles as Insulae Britannicae. Caesar's armies first arrived somewhere near Deal in Kent in 55 BC, but didn't have a lot of luck in establishing a foothold and had to return the following year, when they were able to install a pro-Roman king called Mandubracius. But the Roman army had to retreat once again.

The big Roman invasion took place in AD 43, and the armies made landfall in what is now south-east England, possibly at Rutupiae (now Richborough in Kent) or perhaps Novomagius (now Chichester in West Sussex) or Southampton. The Britons fought the Roman soldiers but were overpowered. The Roman troops began to spread out across their newly conquered kingdom, encountering a great deal of resistance along the way. But they always crushed it.

At this point in Britain's history, the country consisted of many different tribes, each with its own leader. But now Britannia, as it was known to the Romans, was given its first governor – Aulus Plautius, who was one of Emperor Claudius's generals. As the years went on, the Roman conquest of Britain continued. The Romans moved north to Caledonia (what is now Scotland), with mixed success. They built Hadrian's Wall and the Antonine Wall, which were both defensive fortifications.

By the 2nd century, Britannia was represented by a goddess, equipped with a trident and shield, and wearing a helmet. She appeared on some of the coins that were minted at the time, and was shown sitting on a globe above the waves. It's an image that we are still familiar with today.

Although, according to the song 'Rule Britannia', Britannia still rules the waves, the Roman armies stopped ruling Britain in about 410. The reasons for this are still debated – did the Romans have more pressing problems elsewhere or had the Britons got fed up with the

Romans? Either way, the troops were withdrawn, and Britannia was left to its own devices.

Although it was the end of Roman rulership of the islands that became known as the British Isles, other invaders would follow.

THEY CAME FROM THE NORTH

Between the 8th and 11th centuries, northern Europe was held in the grip of a maritime menace – the Vikings. They were highly skilled sailors from Scandinavia who quickly invaded much of the continent. Their reasons for doing this are hotly debated. One theory is that the Vikings were retaliating after Charlemagne and his armies had converted many pagan communities to Christianity, whether they liked it or not. Another theory is that the Vikings had simply run out of space in their homelands and needed to colonise other parts of Europe. And yet another is that they wanted to share in the rich trading possibilities that were on offer.

Regardless of their reasons for setting sail, they had great command of the sea thanks to their brilliant ship designs. Viking longships were designed for raids and exploration, and were equipped with both sails and oars so the ships could keep moving even when no wind was blowing. The longships had shallow drafts, which enabled them to enter shallow waters, such as river estuaries, without any danger of running aground. The other type of Viking ship was the knarr, which was intended for merchant shipping. Its broader hull and deeper draft were designed for carrying cargo.

Some parts of Britain were particular targets for Viking raids. The island of Lindisfarne, which was home to a rich monastery, was first raided in 793. According to the *Anglo-Saxon Chronicle*, which probably dates from the late 9th century, some alarming meteorological events had heralded the first arrival of the Vikings. 'In this year fierce, foreboding omens came over the land of Northumbria. There were excessive whirlwinds, lightning storms, and fiery dragons were seen flying in the sky. These signs were followed by great famine, and on 8 January [thought to be wrongly transcribed, the correct date being 8 June] the ravaging of heathen men destroyed God's church at Lindisfarne.'

A year later, the highly successful (and therefore rich) monastery on the island of Iona, just off the south-west coast of Mull, was raided. After that, repeated raids finally caused its monks to abandon it in 849.

By the middle of the 9th century, Danish Viking armies had conquered huge swathes of England. Northumbria, Mercia and East Anglia were all under Danish rule (their part of the country became known as Danelaw), with only Wessex resisting. While a succession of Danish kings was ruling England, Norwegian Vikings settled in Scotland. For instance, the Orkney Islands were conquered by Harald Hårfagre of Norway in 875 and became a semiautonomous Norwegian earldom until they fell under Scottish rule in 1231 following the murder of the final Norwegian earl.

In the winter of 1013, Sweyn Forkbeard became the first Danish king to rule England – he was King of Denmark, Norway and England. However, a fatal fall from his horse put an end to his rulership almost before it began, and he was succeeded by his younger son, Canute, who reigned in England from 1016–35. There were two more Danish kings, both sons of Canute – Harold I (1035–40) and Hardecnut (1040–42) – before the throne reverted to the Anglo-Saxons in the form of Edward the Confessor (1042–66).

England might have heaved a huge collective sigh of relief when Edward took the throne, but had no idea at the time of his death on 5 January 1066 that it was going to be a very significant year indeed.

PARLEZ-VOUS FRANÇAIS?

If there had been such things as newspapers in 1066, their summing up of the year's events would have run to many pages. Three different kings sat on the English throne in 1066. It was also the year when England was invaded by the Normans. They weren't the first invaders – England had only rid itself of its last Danish king 24 years before – and nor were they the last to arrive in the British Isles. But the Normans' arrival radically changed the English way of life.

So how did it all start? It was largely the result of a lot of dithering on the part of Edward the Confessor, who in 1042 was the first English king to regain the throne after a succession of Danish posteriors had occupied it since the Viking invasions of the 9th century. Although Edward wore the crown, his father-in-law Earl Godwin (after whom the dangerous Goodwin Sands are said to have been named) ran the country, leading to massive tussles between them. Edward relied on a lot of Norman support, which didn't endear him to his subjects. His marriage hadn't produced any children (hardly surprising, as he lived a monastic life) so he had to name his successor. It is believed that in 1051 he bestowed this privilege on his great-nephew, William, Duke of Normandy. But then Earl Godwin died in 1053 and Edward began to rely on Godwin's son, Harold. Just as Godwin had once been the power behind the throne, now that task fell to Harold. Understandably, given the circumstances, there was bad blood between William and Harold, who both had their eye on taking over after Edward died.

At this point it gets more complicated. According to the Bayeux Tapestry and other Norman sources, in 1064 Harold took an oath, in William's presence, to defend William's right to the throne. But when Edward lay dying in January 1066, he is alleged to have named Harold as his successor. Harold immediately took the throne and, obviously not wishing to hang about, got himself crowned on 6 January, the day after Edward had died.

So far, so tangled. Unfortunately, William and Harold weren't the only ones who wanted definitive rulership over England. King Harald III Norway, also wanted to be king of England, and Harold's brother, Tostig, who was in exile, promised to help him.

The timing was everything. The English coast had already been attacked in May 1066 by Tostig and his forces, but they were routed by Harold's militia and Tostig retreated to Scotland. In September, Harald III and Tostig invaded the north of England, with Harold and his army in hot pursuit. They were both killed during the Battle of Stamford Bridge, outside York, on 25 September 1066.

Meanwhile, William was impatiently waiting in France for the wind to change so he and his fleet could sail across the Channel and invade England. He finally set sail on 27 September, while Harold was still busy in the north, and landed at Pevensey (in what is now East Sussex) the following day. He and his troops immediately headed for nearby Hastings. So did Harold and his men, although they were worn out after the Battle of Stamford Bridge.

The two sides met at Senlac Hill, near the town now known as Battle, at dawn on 14 October. The two sides fought all day, until Harold was killed late that afternoon, possibly (although not definitely) after being shot through the eye with an arrow. His part-time soldiers, known as the fyrd, fled, while the professional soldiers, known as housecarls, fought until they dropped. It was later written that the fields had been 'covered in corpses, and all around the only colour to meet the gaze was blood-red'. By this time, the result of the battle was a foregone conclusion. Although there were still pockets of resistance to his arrival in south-east England, William and his troops burnt and pillaged their way through these until they reached London. He was crowned at Westminster Abbey on 25 December 1066.

Four years later, work began to build Battle Abbey on the site of the Battle of Hastings as penance (ordered by Pope Alexander II) for the number of lives lost during the Norman Conquest. The high altar was built on the spot where Harold was said to have fallen. On the one hand, this could be seen as an example of William's piety. Alternatively, it could be viewed as a reminder of the result of the battle – the death of the English king at the hands of the Normans. The Benedictine abbey had a chequered history and is now a ruin, but it and the historic battlefield are open to the public.

Of course, the Norman Conquest brought England a lot more than Battle Abbey. It completely altered the course of English history. It also changed the English language, with the introduction of many French words. It altered the style of English architecture and it revolutionised many customs and laws. Thanks to the outcome of a prolonged battle on an autumn day, England had changed for ever.

THE BARBARY PIRATES

Between the 16th and 18th centuries, there were many menaces at sea. Not only did sailors have to cope with the vagaries of the weather and the difficulties of life onboard but they also had to run the gauntlet of the many pirates who spent their lives plundering ships. Yet there was an even worse danger than ordinary pirates.

The Barbary corsairs, also known as Barbary pirates, were Muslims from North Africa who not only looted ships but took the crew prisoner, treating them with great cruelty as their slaves. Most notorious of all were Hayreddin Barbarossa and Oruç Reis, who were brothers from the Ottoman Empire. Many of the corsairs came from such ports as Algiers and Tunis (known in Britain as the Barbary Coast), having been instructed by their governments to prey on the shipping from Christian countries. And they found rich pickings in British ships. According to records in the Admiralty, the corsairs seized 466 British ships alone between 1609 and 1616.

This was frightening enough, because if you were enslaved by the corsairs and sold on to another master you might never see your homeland again. But then things got much, much worse. Not content with boarding ships at sea, the corsairs became so daring that they took to landing on unprotected stretches of coastline, sneaking into villages and towns under cover of darkness, grabbing any man they could find and making off again before anyone could raise the alarm. It must have sounded like something out of a sinister fairy tale, yet it was all too true. The problems were so bad in Spain and Italy that some parts of their coastlines became almost deserted.

The corsairs found particularly rich pickings off Land's End and the Lizard, even to the point of settling on the island of Lundy at one point in the 17th century. In 1625, 30 of the corsairs' lantern-rigged xebecs were seen off the coast of St Ives in Cornwall, which induced waves of panic in the south-west of England. Naval ships tried and failed to send the corsairs on their way, and churches collected money to pay for the release of newly taken prisoners. This ransom money was put into a central pot administered by the Crown, but it only paid out for the release of some men. The rest were left to their fate, with their women and children having to fend for themselves at home. Twenty-seven British ships were taken from the coast of Plymouth alone in 1625. In 1631 pirates and armed troops stormed the port of Baltimore in County Cork and took away over 100 women and children.

And so it continued. Samuel Pepys recorded a conversation about it in his diary on 8 February 1661. '... to the Fleece tavern to drink and there we spent till 4 a-clock telling stories of Algier and the manner of the life of Slaves there; and truly, Captain Mootham and Mr Dawes (who have been both slaves there) did make me full acquainted with their condition there. As, how they eat nothing but bread and water. At their redemption they pay so much for the water they drink at the public fountains, during their being slaves. How they are beat upon the soles of the feet and bellies at the Liberty of their Padron. How they are at night called into their master's Bagnard, and there they lie.'

There had been numerous peace treaties between England and North Africa from the 1630s onwards but they always broke down sooner or later. Finally, under Charles II, English ships mounted a succession of attacks on Ottoman ports, and peace treaties were signed between England and the Barbary States. Problems flared up again in the 19th century and only ended when Algiers became a French possession in 1830.

'GOD'S WIND BLEW, AND THEY WERE SCATTERED'

Sixteenth-century England had already faced many religious upheavals but in 1588 it encountered a new threat. The Spanish, under their king Philip II, were poised to invade. Not only did Philip want to teach the English a lesson after the way Francis Drake and his ilk had damaged Spanish trading in the Caribbean, he wanted to reverse the Protestant wave that had flooded England and return the country to what he believed to be the only true religion – Roman Catholicism. His late wife, Mary I, had already tried this when she was queen, which had led to persecutions, burnings and widespread fear throughout England. Now her half-sister, Elizabeth I, was on the throne and she'd restored the country to Protestantism and a greater religious tolerance. What's more, she had ordered the execution of Mary, Queen of Scots, who had been her heir to the throne. Mary had been a Roman Catholic. Her son, James VI of Scotland, was a Protestant and would be the next king of England.

Philip announced his intention to invade England in September 1587 with his fleet of ships, which was known as the Armada. Francis Drake and a fleet of English ships retaliated by damaging many Spanish ships at Cadiz. As a result, the Spanish Armada wasn't ready for action until late spring 1588. The plan was for them to sail up from Spain, across the English Channel and up to the Netherlands, where they would collect thousands of infantrymen, before launching their attack on England. They knew this was risky because although the Spanish had a bigger army and a greater number of ships, the English had much better ships with powerful, long-range guns. England prepared for battle. And waited.

On 29 July 1588 the Spanish fleet was glimpsed off the coast of Plymouth. A complex network of beacons was lit all over southern England to warn of imminent invasion. After a week of skirmishes that resolved nothing, the Spanish anchored off Gravelines on what was then the Flemish coast, and the English launched their fireships at them. These were ageing ships that were smeared with pitch, loaded with flammable material such as brimstone, and then set alight. This terrifying attack broke the Spanish lines and led to the Battle of Gravelines on 8 August. The wind was against the Spanish ships but then it shifted and the Armada had no choice but to go where the wind blew them, which was into the North Sea. From there, the Armada sailed up the east coast of England and round Scotland before heading into the North Atlantic.

The Spanish sailors didn't know this coastline and many of the ships were wrecked on the rocks they encountered en route. A contemporary account by Camden in *Annales Rerum Angliae et Hiberniae Regnante Elizabetha* described the Armada's plight as having been 'driven round about all Britaine, by Scotland, the Orcades, and Ireland, most grievously tossed, and very much distressed and wasted by stormes, wrackes, and all kind of miseries.'

It was the cause of much rejoicing in England. Elizabeth gave her famous victory speech at Tilbury docks in which she expressed her 'foul scorn that Parma or Spain, or any Prince of Europe, should dare to invade the border of my realm'.

Medals were struck in celebration, bearing a succinct Latin inscription on the front that, when translated, read 'God's wind blew, and they were scattered'. The reverse read 'I [the Church of England] am assailed not injured'. The entire episode had been a tremendous triumph for the British Navy, and also for the new religion. Because God's wind was considered to be a Protestant one.

MARTELLO TOWERS

If you visit the south-east coast of England between East Sussex and Kent, or between Essex and Suffolk in East Anglia, you may see some strange buildings that look like huge sandcastles created with a giant's bucket and spade. These are Martello towers – defensive fortifications that were built between 1805 and 1808 in the hope that they would prevent Napoleon Bonaparte invading the British Isles. In the event, they weren't necessary because 'Boney' never made it over the Channel. However, they did come in handy during the Second World War when once again Britain was at risk of invasion. Today many of the towers have vanished or been incorporated into other buildings, but some are still standing.

Each tower was circular, with very thick brick walls that were intended to resist cannon fire and a flat roof armed with a single cannon mounted on a swivelling platform that gave it a panoramic view of the enemy approaching. The door was halfway up the side of the building, and only accessible by a ladder. Each tower had living quarters for up to 24 men and one officer.

Originally there were 103 of them, and each one bore a number for easy identification by the British army. Between 1805 and 1808, 74 towers were built at regular intervals along the coast from Folkestone (the site of tower No. 1) in Kent down to Seaford (the site of tower No. 74) in what is now East Sussex. Building work resumed in 1809 with a string of towers along the East Anglian coast. These were larger and more heavily fortified because the French would have been able to use bigger ships if they had invaded this stretch of coastline. The 29 towers, which were identified by letters of the alphabet to distinguish them from their more southerly cousins, ran from St Osyth (the site of tower A) in Essex to Slaughden (tower CC), just south of Aldeburgh in Suffolk.

Southern England isn't the only preserve of the Martello tower. Three were built in Scotland between 1813 and 1815: one on the rocks off Leith Harbour in the Firth of Forth, and two near Longhope in the Orkney Islands. Thirty towers were also built on Jersey in the Channel Islands, although these look very different from those on the British mainland because they are taller and were built from local granite rather than brick.

Occupation

In the early summer of 1940 as the Second World War really began to bite, the British government was facing a difficult decision. What should it do about the defence of the Channel Islands? Their position off the northern coast of Nazi-occupied France made them acutely vulnerable to attack, but as they had no strategic importance to Britain it was decided that there was no reason to spend valuable resources in defending them.

Any Channel Islander who wanted to leave was evacuated in the greatest secrecy during June 1940, but two-thirds of the population decided to stay put and face whatever fate was going to bring them.

Destiny arrived on 28 June when the Luftwaffe bombed Guernsey and Jersey, killing 44 people. Hitler's Operation Green Arrow – the plan to occupy the Channel Islands – had begun. Two days later, the Germans arrived in person when the Luftwaffe took control of Guernsey's airfield. The chief of police, who greeted them, assured them that the islands were undefended. The German flag was raised the following day, and then Jersey was occupied too, followed by Alderney and Sark over the next couple of days.

The Germans erected four concentration camps on Alderney, two of which housed the slave labour needed to build massive fortifications and other defences on the islands. They built underground hospitals on Jersey and Guernsey, which are now open to the public, and took command of the local prisons. All the Channel Islanders were banned from listening to the radio, although many did so in secret as an act of passive resistance. The time zone was switched from Greenwich Mean Time to Central European Time, and the traffic was also brought in line with continental Europe so the islanders had to get used to driving on the right instead of the left.

It was a very difficult and frightening time for the islanders. The ratio of islanders to German soldiers was roughly two to one, so many felt it was dangerous to engage in anything other than small acts of rebellion. Others risked their lives to harbour escaped prisoners and to defy the German occupation in a host of different ways. During the occupation more than 300 islanders were taken from Jersey alone to prisons and concentration camps in Europe, and not all of them came home again.

France was liberated from German occupation in 1944 but the Allies decided they couldn't liberate the Channel Islands because they were so heavily fortified. The liberation of France meant that the Germans could no longer supply the Channel Islands with food, so both the islanders and the occupying German army began to go hungry.

Relief finally arrived on 8 May 1945, when war in Europe ended and the Channel Islands were freed. The following morning, the German army surrendered unconditionally onboard HMS *Bulldog*, which had sailed into St Peter Port in Guernsey. Similar scenes took place onboard HMS *Beagle* in Jersey. The nightmare was finally over.

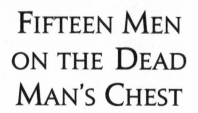

FIFTEEN MEN
ON THE DEAD
MAN'S CHEST

The fire-flash shines from Reculver cliff,
And the answering light burns blue in the skiff

THE INGOLDSBY LEGENDS, 'THOMAS INGOLDSBY'
(THE REV. RICHARD H BARHAM)

PIRATES!

Hollywood's classic idea of a pirate is a tall, handsome man with dazzling white teeth, a magnificent beard and dashing clothes that show off his perfect legs and body. He's a swashbuckling, cutlass-wielding, romantic figure who usually gets the girl in the final reel. And his piratical activities are normally confined to derring-do with dastardly baddies who deserve everything they get, which might include being made to walk the plank.

Real pirates, especially those from the classic age of piracy between the 1680s and the 1720s, were a rather different kettle of fish. Film-star good looks were a rarity. Instead, the average pirate was likely to be short, with rotting (or missing) teeth, skin badly scarred by smallpox and other ailments and eye problems such as a squint. These men (and occasionally women) were far from being pin-ups.

So who were they? Pirates came from many walks of life. Some sailors decided it was the only way of keeping body and soul together after being released from service at the end of a war. Other sailors preferred a life of piracy to the punishing and gruelling job of fishing around Newfoundland. Some were on the make, hoping to secure their fortunes. Others were sailors who'd mutinied on merchant ships when conditions became intolerable. And then there were the slaves who'd been captured while on slave ships and had little choice in the matter. Perhaps they felt that their lives couldn't get any worse.

One of the great attractions of piracy was that conditions onboard were egalitarian, in stark contrast to naval and merchant ships. Everyone shared in the plunder that was seized and sailors who were injured in battle received financial help. Everyone knew the rules, although whether they abided by them was another matter.

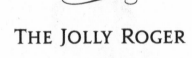

THE JOLLY ROGER

Although it sounds like the name of a cheerful pub, the Jolly Roger was the name given to the flag flown to identify a pirate's ship. It could be of any design, provided that it was sufficiently menacing to strike terror into the hearts of any ship's crew that spotted it coming towards them. The hope was that they'd surrender without putting up much of a fight. It's highly unlikely that the poor crews, knees knocking like castanets, thought there was anything jolly about the flag looming out of the mists.

The classic Jolly Roger design shows a skull and crossbones: a human skull floating above two crossed bones against a black background. This was the chosen ensign of several notorious pirates, although others preferred to create their own variations, which ranged from an hourglass (time is running out and death is close) to crossed cutlasses to the Devil himself. A logbook dated 6 December 1687, and now held in the Bibliothèque Nationale de France, is thought to contain the first description of the flag, although in this case the skull and crossbones had a red background.

The name 'Jolly Roger' was probably first used in 1724, when it appeared in *A General History of the Pyrates* by a man calling himself Charles Johnson (although he might have been Daniel Defoe in disguise). How did it get its name? It may be a corruption of the French phrase *jolie rouge* (meaning 'pretty red'), which was the name given to a plain red flag that was hoisted to show that the crew would fight until no man was left standing.

Flags are carried onboard ship in order to signal where the ship has come from and to reduce confusion as much as possible. In the middle of the 18th century, black pirate flags indicated that the crew would show mercy. Red or bloody flags, on the other hand, were self-evident. No quarter would be given, no mercy shown, and it would be every man for himself.

BIG BAD BLACKBEARD

History loves characters who are larger than life. The meek and boring ones are usually forgotten, but how can we ignore a man who allegedly liked frightening his enemies by tying lighted fuses beneath his hat?

He gained his soubriquet because of his luxuriant black beard, which he would tie in plaits secured with ribbons. What was his real name? Rather fittingly, bearing in mind that we're talking about someone who combines glamour with notoriety, we aren't sure. Blackbeard may have been born Edward Teach (or possibly Thatch) in Bristol in about 1680. There again, he might not, because pirates had good reason to change their surnames in order to protect their families' honour and reputation. The fact that no one is sure who he really was only adds to the glamour of the pirate popularly known as Blackbeard.

What is more certain about Blackbeard is that he gained an early apprenticeship as a pirate when he joined forces with Benjamin Hornigold in the Bahamas in 1714 or 1715. Hornigold was a successful pirate with a crew of about 70 men, but they eventually deposed him. Blackbeard, on the other hand, went from strength to strength.

In November 1717 he captured a French slave ship off Martinique and renamed it *Queen Anne's Revenge*. He had a fleet of ships and a massive crew of over 150 men who he apparently managed to control very well, partly by creating a fearsome persona that deterred anyone from causing trouble. There are lurid tales of him setting his men dangerous challenges, such as the time he took a few men down into the ship's hold, set fire to some brimstone and waited there to see who escaped first. He was delighted to be the last man out. He is also alleged to have said that he had to periodically kill one of his crew in order to remind them who he was.

Being a notorious pirate was a tricky business, and after a succession of adventures Blackbeard finally met his match. He and his men had accepted a pardon from the Governor of North Carolina, but they had continued to work as pirates. This had to be stopped, and on 22 November 1718 Blackbeard was killed at Ocracoke Inlet in North Carolina during a battle with the Royal Navy. As with so many other aspects of Blackbeard's life, there are differing accounts of his death. One says that he was repeatedly peppered with musket shot yet managed to continue wielding his cutlass until he finally fell down dead. Another claims that he was beheaded. Either way, he was eventually decapitated, with his body slung into the water and his head attached to the bowsprit of one of the Navy sloops so its captain could claim the handsome reward that had been posted for Blackbeard's death.

Blackbeard may have been killed but, according to many superstitious sailors, his spirit lives on. Lights that are seen at sea but don't have any rational explanation are often referred to as 'Teach's lights'. There is also the bloodcurdling story that Blackbeard's skull was turned into a drinking vessel. He also lives on as the inspiration of many characters in seafaring stories. In 1997 what is thought to be the wreckage of his ship, *Queen Anne's Revenge*, was located and excavated, and many of the objects found onboard are now displayed at the North Carolina Maritime Museum.

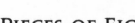

PIECES OF EIGHT

'Pieces of eight! Pieces of eight!' It's a classic phrase for pirates, and was even squawked by Long John Silver's parrot in *Treasure Island*, written by Robert Louis Stevenson. But what does the phrase actually refer to?

It was the Spanish dollar, a piece of currency that had a powerful impact on other nations, even to the point of the US dollar being founded on it. Its correct Spanish name was *real de a ocho*, which translated as the 'eight reale coin'. It was made of silver and was minted in the Spanish Empire after the Spanish currency was reformed in 1497. The coin was widely used across the known world, and only stopped being legal tender in the US in 1857.

No wonder pirates (and their parrots) were so keen to get their hands on it.

CUSTOMS AND CONTRABAND

When Edward I hit on the bright idea of imposing customs duties in 1275 (£3 on a bag of wool exported from England) in order to finance his many military campaigns, his English subjects began to think up ways of outwitting this new tax. They were even more determined to do this from 1303, when Edward negotiated to impose similar duties on foreign merchants. At this stage, the customs duties only concerned the import and export of wool. That was bad enough, since England was a country of sheep-breeders and wool-exporters, but worse was to come. As successive kings thought up new ways of raising much-needed revenue, all sorts of essential items became subject to customs duties, including grain, tea and hides for making leather, while more luxurious goods such as silk, lace, wine and spirits were also taxed. Some of these duties were short-lived but others, such as the tax on tea and wool, endured for many years. Which meant, of course, that there was a roaring trade in smuggling them in and out of the country.

Some parts of the British coastline were more suitable for smuggling than others. Smugglers needed plenty of places to hide their contraband, not only when it was leaving the country but also when it was coming in from abroad. They also needed areas that were treacherous for the customs men who were trying to catch them, so steep cliffs, marshland and places that offered other natural hazards were ideal. No wonder that Romney Marsh in Kent, with its boggy land and frequent dykes, was a hotbed of smuggling activity. So was Cornwall, because its wild and rocky coastline is pockmarked with useful caves and other hidey-holes. Something else that the smugglers needed was access to a ready market, so they either had to be able to reach large cities and towns easily or they had to sell the goods locally. It helped if everyone in the district was involved in smuggling, whether they financed it or received the contraband, as this dramatically reduced the likelihood of whistleblowers blabbing to the authorities.

No one wanted to be caught smuggling, as the punishment could be severe. The death penalty was already in force (it had been introduced in 1662 for smuggling wool), but a law passed in 1746 put a bounty of £500 on a smuggler's head. And now it wasn't only the smuggler who was punished but anyone else involved in the smuggling too. If a smuggler was convicted of killing a customs officer, his body was left hanging from a gibbet for everyone to see.

Such draconian punishments succeeded in tempering smuggling, but not in the way the authorities had intended. Smugglers now faced such terrible punishments that they couldn't risk being discovered, so they were merciless towards anyone who posed a threat. Their resulting thuggery, viciousness and cold-bloodedness was so appalling that they gradually lost the local support on which they depended. It wasn't the end of smuggling, but smugglers were no longer regarded as harmless free-booters who were helping the local economy, but became men to be feared.

A Smuggler's Song

It was not a good move to see the smugglers in action, as this poem by Rudyard Kipling describes.

If you wake at Midnight, and hear a horse's feet,
Don't go drawing back the blind, or looking in the street.
Them that ask no questions isn't told a lie.
Watch the wall, my darling, while the Gentlemen go by!

Five and twenty ponies,
Trotting through the dark –
Brandy for the Parson,
'Baccy for the Clerk;
Laces for a lady, letters for a spy,
And watch the wall, my darling, while the Gentlemen go by!

Running round the woodlump, if you chance to find
Little barrels, roped and tarred, all full of brandy-wine,
Don't you shout to come and look, nor use 'em for your play.
Put the brushwood back again – and they'll be gone next day!

If you see the stable door setting open wide;
If you see a tired horse lying down inside;
If your mother mends a coat cut about and tore;
If the lining's wet and warm – don't you ask no more!

If you meet King George's men, dressed in blue and red,
You be careful what you say, and mindful what is said.
If they call you 'pretty maid', and chuck you 'neath the chin,
Don't you tell where no one is, nor yet where no one's been!

Knocks and footsteps round the house – whistles after dark –
You've no call for running out till the house-dogs bark.
Trusty's here, and *Pincher's* here, and see how dumb they lie –
They don't fret to follow when the Gentlemen go by!

If you do as you've been told, 'likely there's a chance,
You'll be given a dainty doll, all the way from France,
With a cap of Valenciennes, and a velvet hood –
A present from the Gentlemen, along o' being good!

Five and twenty ponies,
Trotting through the dark –
Brandy for the Parson,
'Baccy for the Clerk;
Them that asks no questions isn't told a lie –
Watch the wall, my darling, while the Gentlemen go by!

WRECKERS!

It wasn't only smugglers who benefitted illegally from living on or near the coast, wreckers benefitted too. Most of them simply waited for ships to founder before helping themselves to the goods that were washed ashore.

Everyone living nearby would get in on the act when a ship was wrecked. Many people in the West Country in the 17th and 18th centuries endured a hand-to-mouth existence, relying on dangerous activities such as tin mining for their living. Any extra food, drink or clothing that was washed up on the beach was a much-needed bonus. Not that the reviled customs officers saw it like that, since anything that was found was supposed to be declared at the nearest customs house. But there was little chance of that happening. Instead, the wreck would be picked clean, even to the point of breaking it up for firewood.

Anyone wanting to help themselves to a wreck's cargo had to be quick off the mark, otherwise nothing would be left by the time they got to the beach. And wreckage could be washed up at any time. The story goes that one Sunday morning the vicar of the village of Portlemouth was droning his way through a sleep-inducing sermon when the door of the church burst open. A man entered and went up to the pulpit, where he whispered in the vicar's ear. Apparently, the vicar promptly threw off his surplice, announced that a ship had run aground and, together with the rest of the congregation, who'd woken up by that time, raced down to the shore.

Whether wreckers deliberately lured ships on to the rocks is a hotly disputed point. Is it the stuff of legend or is there a grain of truth in it? According to local legend, it really happened at Morte Point in North Devon. It was home to the local smugglers, known as Mortemen, who were feared for good reason. The story goes that on dark nights in wild weather they would tie lanterns to the tails of their mules, then lead them around the top of Morte Point. Any ships out at sea would mistake the lanterns for the safe lights of port and sail towards them, only to be smashed against the rocks. The Mortemen would then race down to the shore to kill off any members of the crew who hadn't drowned before plundering the goods onboard. Their escapades finally ended in 1879, thanks to the building of a lighthouse at nearby Bull Point.

On a Hiding to Something

If you were a smuggler or a wrecker who wanted to hide your contraband from prying eyes or the strong arm of the law, you had to be inventive. You never knew when the excisemen would turn up to investigate, so you had to be quick as well.

Smugglers importing barrels often hid them in the false bottoms of their boats. But what did they do with them when they reached land? Caves might offer a temporary hiding place but they had many disadvantages, such as filling with water at high tide and dashing the plunder against the rocks. Anywhere that was too easy to get at was likely to be discovered by the authorities in no time at all. One perfect option was to hide the contraband in the sea, and barrels were often lashed together with a sandbag at one end to act as an anchor and an inflated bladder and a bundle of feathers at the other to mark the source of the loot. The smugglers used four-armed grapplers, which they called 'creepers', to retrieve the submerged barrels. There was always the danger that the seawater would infiltrate poorly made barrels, making their contents undrinkable. Ruined French brandy was known as 'stinky-booze' in the West Country.

It was much easier to hide smaller items of contraband. Lace, gloves and tea could all be divided up into small parcels, and many smugglers wore these underneath their clothes. Tobacco was sometimes plaited into the rigging of the smugglers' ships.

A smuggler couldn't relax even when they'd got their contraband safely ashore, because they still had to hide it until it could be distributed or sold. While they were on their travels, they would grease their horses' coats to make it difficult for the excisemen to get hold of them. Many houses in noted smuggling areas had useful hidey-holes, such as false cupboards and hidden staircases. Contraband was often hidden in secret compartments beneath windows. Even churches were used as good hiding places, and many of them had a tunnel that ran to the local pub.

The one thing you didn't want if you were a smuggler was to attract lots of attention. In fact, sometimes it was in your interest to deter it, and one way to do that was to create hair-raising stories of ghosts. It may well be that some legends about local ghosts are certainly connected with spirits, but they are more likely to be the sort that come in barrels rather than those unquiet souls that walk at night. One good wheeze was to make the most of this by hiding contraband in a churchyard, as most people were keen to keep away from such places. The large table tombs in churchyards were ideal for this, because who in their right mind would want to look inside them?

Smugglers not only needed to know where to hide their loot but they also needed to know which places welcomed them and which posed a threat. There were numerous signs to show that somewhere was friendly towards the free-booters, as smugglers were often known. For instance, lime trees planted outside an inn indicated a safe haven for smugglers, as did somewhere that displayed an image of a dolphin. A picture of a ship, especially if it was painted on the wall of somewhere unlikely, such as a church, was another indication that a smuggler would be safe.

DESPERADOES

Smuggling in the 17th and 18th centuries could be a heartless business. It was often every man for himself, and with the death penalty already assured for anyone found guilty of smuggling there was every reason to kill anyone who might be in danger of alerting the authorities to what was going on. What's more, it was in the smugglers' interests to create a ruthless, bloodthirsty image that would leave everyone in their thrall. As a result, some gangs of smugglers really took this to heart.

The Hawkhurst Gang

One of the most notorious gangs was known as the Hawkhurst Gang. They flourished during the 18th and 19th centuries, running their operations from the Oak and Ivy Pub in Hawkhurst in Kent. At one point, they claimed to be able to muster 500 men within a couple of hours. They ran a highly profitable smuggling ring that ferried contraband on packhorses from Romney Marsh in Kent, through Hawkhurst and up to London. These men were feared, and for good reason because they showed no mercy. Rival gangs had to obey their orders or face the consequences. Members of the Hawkhurst Gang were so confident of their power that they sometimes displayed their weapons quite openly: they once outraged many people in Rye when they had a drink in the window of the Mermaid Inn and left their pistols on the table. The fact that the pistols were cocked, ready for action, didn't help. A posse of 20 of them also visited the nearby Red Lion Pub, where they fired their pistols at the ceiling for fun and to assert their authority.

The Hawkhurst Gang saw nothing wrong in getting rid of anyone who stood in their way or who posed a threat. They relieved excisemen of their weapons when necessary, terrorised the locals into keeping quiet about their activities and flexed their muscles in brawls and fights with rival gangs.

These men were definitely not the sort you want to meet in a dark alley, but they weren't the only smuggling gang who made the most of their power to frighten people.

∽ Thomas Knight ∽

In the late 18th century, Barry Island in Wales really was an island. It was also the domain of a smuggler called Thomas Knight who was operating a highly profitable business importing tobacco and spirits from the Channel Islands and soap from Ireland. He put up fortified defences around the island and exercised such control over the locals that the customs men found it hard to recruit new members. Despite this, Barry Island became too hot for him in 1785 and he retreated to the island of Lundy. Another smuggler called William Arthur quickly stepped into his shoes, and was as big a thorn in the side of the authorities as his predecessor.

∽ The King of Prussia ∽

Cornwall was a thriving area for smugglers, and one of the most notorious was a family who were collectively known as the Carters of

Prussia Cove. They operated around Mount's Bay (a major smuggling area) near Cudden Point from the late 18th century. Originally, Prussia Cove was called Porthleah, but it got its current name because John Carter, the head of the gang, styled himself 'the King of Prussia'. He worked with his two brothers, Harry and Charles, and lived in a house that stood on the headland of Prussia Bay.

This was good cover for his smuggling activities and gave him plenty of scope for inventive opportunism, such as mounting a battery of guns on the cliffs. He claimed these were to protect him from French privateers although it's more likely they were intended to deter excisemen from sticking their noses into his business. Interestingly, John and Harry Carter were both devout Methodists. They even banned swearing on their two boats and, allegedly, Harry held Sunday services on the quayside at Roscoff when he was exiled there.

There is no record of John's activities after 1807 and Harry eventually became a full-time preacher, but other members of the family continued the smuggling tradition until a coastguard station was built at Prussia Cove in 1825, thereby snuffing out all activity at a stroke.

MOONRAKERS AND OWLERS

Smugglers had to come up with all sorts of inventive ways of eluding the excisemen who were continually trying to catch them.

❧ Moonrakers ❧

Stories abound but one of the most celebrated concerns a gang of smugglers in the village of Bishops Cannings in Wiltshire. One moonlit night they were trying to rake out barrels of spirits that they'd hidden in the village pond when some excisemen arrived. When the smugglers were asked what they were doing, they pointed to the moon's reflection in the pond and pretended that they thought it was a big cheese. They said they were trying to rake it out of the pond. Convinced that they were talking to a gang of village idiots, the excisemen shook their heads in amused disbelief and went on their way. The name stuck, and the inhabitants of Wiltshire are still sometimes known as 'Moonrakers'.

❧ Owlers ❧

On Romney Marsh in Kent, smugglers were known as 'owlers'. No one is sure why they got this name although there are several suggestions. Was it because they operated by night and communicated with each other by imitating the sound of owls; or was 'owler' a corruption of 'wooler', as their main trade was wool? These smugglers were kept busy for centuries, as they operated in one of the biggest wool-producing parts of Britain. Owlers were doubly lucky because not only did they have the run of the isolated and inhospitable marsh but they also benefited from being near several ports of the time, including Rye and Lydd (now landlocked).

❧ The Battle of Brookland ❧

Customs officers knew what smugglers were up to. But catching them was the problem, partly because the customs officers were often totally outnumbered. There were even pitched battles between smugglers and the excisemen. One, involving 200 members of the Aldington Gang, took place early in the morning of 11 February 1821. Excisemen caught the gang red-handed at Camber as they unloaded 1,000 gallons of Geneva gin and 1,000 gallons of brandy.

The resulting fight took them right across the marsh to the village of Brookland, and therefore became known as the Battle of Brookland.

Cephas Quested, the leader of the Aldington Gang, was captured when he mistook a naval officer for one of his own men. He handed the man a musket with the injunction to 'take this and blow some officer's brains out'. This costly mistake resulted in Quested being hanged at Newgate Prison in London on 4 July of the same year.

THE SENIOR SERVICE

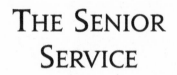

Take my drum to England, hang et by the shore.
Strike et when your powder's runnin' low;
If the Dons sight Devon, I'll quit the port o' Heaven
An' drum them up the Channel as we drummed
them long ago.

'DRAKE'S DRUM', SIR HENRY NEWBOLT

You're in the Navy Now

The Royal Navy is an indissoluble part of British life, yet it is impossible to pinpoint its exact beginnings. Early forms of the British Navy ebbed and flowed like the tide on which it sailed, because fleets of ships were assembled when the need arose and disbanded when they had done their duty. It's the oldest of the UK's three armed services, which is why it's called the Senior Service.

It is sometimes claimed that King Alfred the Great was the founder of the Navy, because he spearheaded a seaborne defence against the Danes in 882 and again in 895–97. Many other kings also contributed to the nation's seafaring history. Edward the Confessor founded the Cinque Ports in the 11th century, which allowed merchant vessels to band together in protection of the country. King John developed a naval base at Portsmouth in the 13th century. Edward III was called 'The King of the Sea' after commanding the English fleet at the Battle of Sluys in 1340 against the combined fleet of the French, Genoese and Castilians. In the 15th century, Henry V ordered the building of the *Jesus*, which was the first ship of 1,000 tons, and the *Grace Dieu*, which at 1,400 tons was the largest ship of its day. And so it went on.

The development of the Navy gathered momentum during the reign of the Tudors. This was the start of the age of exploration and expansion, but the Tudors were also a royal dynasty built on shaky foundations that had to be strengthened if it was going to survive. Enter Henry VIII, who took over seven warships that had been built by his father, Henry VII, and increased that number to 24. The ship *Henry Grace à Dieu*, named for Henry VIII, was launched in 1514 and at the time was the largest warship in the world. It had 122 guns and led to new techniques in maritime warfare. Henry became known as the 'Father of the English Navy', because not only did he found Trinity House in 1514 to provide navigational help to sailors, but he oversaw the creation of the first naval dock in Britain, when one was built in Portsmouth in 1540, and he created the Navy Board in 1546. During the reign of Elizabeth I, the Spanish Armada in 1588 was another test for the Navy, which was led by Lord Howard of Effingham, with Francis Drake as his second-in-command.

Until now, the Navy was called the British Navy. It changed its name to the Royal Navy after the restoration of the monarchy in 1660, when Charles II returned from exile in France to take the throne. Samuel Pepys, the 17th-century diarist whose work with the Navy Board did so much to turn the Navy from a corrupt and chaotic collection of ships into a highly organised and efficient national fleet, wrote that Charles 'best understands the business of the sea of any prince the world ever had'. Pepys attended to everything, from improving the sailors' diet as far as he was able to introducing a system of exams for hopeful lieutenants.

Successive regimes did their bit at improving and modernising the Navy in line with the times. In 1801 the Admiralty produced its first hydrographic chart and in 1819 it was given permission to sell its charts to the Merchant Marine. Since then, almost all navigation of the world's seas has been carried out using British Admiralty charts.

The Navy Board was merged with the Admiralty in 1832 and in 1853 it became possible for sailors to make a career out of the Navy and receive a pension when they retired. The Navy continued to grow and develop so as to keep up with the changes in ship design – not to mention the invention of aircraft. The Royal Naval Air Service (RNAS) was formed in 1912, and merged with the Royal Flying Corps in 1918 to form the Royal Air Force. This was a huge blow to the Navy. The Fleet Air Arm arrived in 1924 and came under control of the Admiralty in May 1939.

The Navy played an important role in both world wars, when male sailors were joined by women for the first time. Women belonged to the Women's Royal Naval Service (WRNS) until it was disbanded in 1993, when women were allowed to become part of the structure of the Royal Navy itself. The only restriction placed on female personnel is that they are not allowed to serve on submarines or with the Royal Marine Commandos. What would Pepys and Charles II, who were both noted for their appreciation of women, have to say about such a turn of events?

THE PRIDE OF THE LINE

Some ships have almost been forgotten, while others have remained in the nation's consciousness long after they rotted away, were blown up by enemy action or were retired from service as a result of government cuts. Here are some of the Royal Navy's ships whose names have echoed down the centuries.

❧ Mary Rose ❧

Today you can see what remains of the *Mary Rose* at Portsmouth Dockyard. She is a miracle of expert salvage work and round-the-clock care, but she is a far cry from her original state. This iconic Tudor warship was one of the first ships that Henry VIII had built when he became king in 1509. He needed to increase the size of his Navy in order to combat threats from the French and the Scots. *Mary Rose* was built in oak and elm, and completed in 1511, probably in Portsmouth. It is thought that her name was an amalgam of that of Henry's favourite sister, Mary, and the Tudor emblem of the rose. She was equipped with streamers and banners, and became the fleet's flagship. *Mary Rose* was one of the first ships to fire a broadside – the simultaneous firing of guns from one side of a ship.

Henry had quite a tempestuous reign and *Mary Rose* saw plenty of action. Her role as the Navy's flagship was eventually taken over by *Henry Grace à Dieu*, but she was still part of the fleet. That ended on 19 July 1545, when she sank during the Battle of the Solent against the French. Attempts to raise her began almost immediately but failed and were eventually abandoned.

Renewed interest in finding her began in 1965 and she was finally raised in 1982, timber by timber, and put together again. What had begun as an amateur hunt for her became a fascinating and highly skilled salvage operation.

⚓ HMS Victory ⚓

The Royal Navy has named six of its ships HMS *Victory*, but we all know which one we're talking about when we mention her name. It is number six, the flagship of the Navy during the Napoleonic Wars and the ship on which Admiral Lord Nelson met his death. She had a long and noble period of service, and her name is still synonymous with bravery in the face of battle.

Like two of her predecessors, she was built as a 100-gun first-rate ship of the line. She was designed by Thomas Slade, the Senior Surveyor of the Navy, and work began on her on 23 July 1759 at Chatham. She was launched there on 7 May 1765. She was made of wood, 90 per cent of which was oak. Her hull was made from oak, fir and elm; her masts and yards were made from pine and spruce; and a huge piece of teak was used for her keel. All this timber had been seasoned for the past 14 years, which greatly contributed to her long life. She was put into 'ordinary' (reserve) and laid up for the next 13 years until she was commissioned on 8 May 1778. In March 1780 her hull was sheeted with copper, as part of the Navy's new practice to counteract shipworm and other growths.

She was the flagship of a succession of admirals, starting with Admiral Keppel, and took part in the American War of Independence. In 1797 she was involved in the Battle of Cape St

Vincent against the Spanish and when she returned to Portsmouth she was assessed as being unfit for service and orders were given for her to be turned into a hospital ship. But not for long. When another ship of the line was lost, she was given extensive repairs and also modernised. Finally, she was ready for action again in 1803.

She sailed out of Portsmouth on 16 May 1803 under the command of Lord Nelson, who had just been appointed commander-in-chief. The Napoleonic Wars had begun and France was threatening to invade Britain. The *Victory* saw plenty of action, leading up to the day with which she is indissolubly linked. On 21 October 1805 Nelson's 27 ships took part in the Battle of Trafalgar, off Cape Trafalgar in Spain. The British routed the French fleet but Nelson was fatally wounded and died below deck. The *Victory* took his body home, arriving in Portsmouth on 4 December 1805. After undergoing repairs at Chatham, she was recommissioned and saw another four years of action in the Baltic and off the Spanish coast, before finally being paid off on 20 December 1812. She was put back into 'ordinary' and in 1824 she became the flagship for the Port Admiral in Portsmouth.

She has remained there ever since, and between 1922 and 1928 was restored to her appearance during the Battle of Trafalgar. She is the flagship of the Second Sea Lord and is kept in No. 2 Dry Dock at Portsmouth's Royal Naval Dockyard, where she is open to the public who still flock to admire her. It is a fitting end for a splendid ship.

Just for the record, these are her five predecessors:

1 Originally the *Great Christopher*, a gun ship bought by the Royal Navy in 1569 and broken up in 1608.
2 Launched at Deptford in 1620. She was a 42-gun great ship (one of the largest ships of the time). She was rebuilt in 1666 and broken up in 1691.
3 Launched in 1675 as the *Royal James* and renamed in March 1691. She was a 100-gun first-rate ship of the line and was accidentally destroyed in a fire in 1721.
4 A 100-gun first-rate ship of the line launched in 1737. She was wrecked in 1744.
5 An eight-gun schooner launched in 1764.

HMS Ark Royal

This is another celebrated name for a Royal Navy ship. There have been five ships named *Ark Royal*, but they've played a very different role to that of the *Victory*, as three of them have been aircraft carriers.

The original *Ark Royal* was one of the most famous ships of her time. She was originally ordered for Sir Walter Raleigh in 1586 and bore the name *Ark Raleigh*. At the time, it was the convention for ships to be named after their owners, so when Elizabeth I bought her the following year she was given the new name of *Ark Royal*. She became the flagship of Charles Howard, 1st Earl of Nottingham, who was England's Lord High Admiral, and was at the head of the English fleet when they chased the Spanish Armada into the North Sea and up towards Scotland in 1588. When James I succeeded to the English throne after Elizabeth's death, he renamed the ship *Anne Royal* in 1608 in honour of his consort, Anne of Denmark. *Anne Royal* became the flagship of Lord Wimbledon, and she remained in service until April 1636, when she was seriously damaged after striking her own anchor. It would have cost so much to repair her that she was finally broken up in 1638.

Just under 300 years later, another ship was given her celebrated name. This ship was being built as a tramp steamer when the Navy bought her in May 1914 and converted her into an aircraft carrier named HMS *Ark Royal*. She was involved in the Allied landings at the Dardanelles in early 1915 and served in various international crises. She was renamed HMS *Pegasus* in December 1934 so that her illustrious name could be given to a new aircraft carrier that was being built.

Her new namesake, HMS *Ark Royal* (91), was launched in April 1937 and had an innovative design. She was able to carry a large number of aircraft, which made her tremendously useful during the Second World War. She was torpedoed by a German submarine on 13 November 1941 off Gibraltar and sank the next day.

The fourth *Ark Royal* was ordered in 1942 but wasn't commissioned until 1955. She was originally going to be called *Irresistible* but the Navy changed this, and her official name became HMS *Ark Royal*

(R09). She was the first British aircraft carrier to be built with angled flight decks and steam catapults, rather than to have these added later. She was scrapped in 1980.

The fifth ship to bear the name of *Ark Royal* was launched in 1981. Originally, she was going to be called HMS *Indomitable*, but she gained her new name because there was so much public resentment at the scrapping of the previous *Ark Royal*. She was the last Invincible-class light aircraft carrier to be built, and was decommissioned in late 2010 because of government spending cuts. Her official title was HMS *Ark Royal* (R07).

In each case, the information in brackets after the ship's name is her pennant number, so she can be specifically identified.

FIRST-RATE!

Today when we describe something as being 'first-rate' we mean it's the very best of its type. Something that is second-rate is infe-rior, and even more so if we call it 'third-rate'. As with so many other phrases that have entered the English language, it originates from the Navy. Actually, to be more precise, it originates from Samuel Pepys who, as First Secretary to the Admiralty in 1677, drew up a rating system for the Navy's ships based on the number of guns they carried. This in turn determined the size of the crew.

First-rate battleships were very expensive to construct so they comprised a very small proportion of the Royal Navy's fleet. This was the rating system used during the Napoleonic Wars.

First rate	100+ guns	850–875 crew
Second rate	90–98 guns	700–750 crew
Third rate	64–84 guns	500–700 crew
Fourth rate	44–54 guns	300–400 crew
Fifth rate	32–40 guns	250 crew
Sixth rate	24–28 guns	200 crew

Ships that were classified as first-, second-, third- or fourth-rate were called 'ships of the line', which meant they were warships that formed a column in order to fire broadsides at the enemy. This was a tactic known as 'line of battle'. Fifth- and sixth-rate warships were too small to take part in line of battle but were valued for their speediness and manoeuvrability, and were known as 'frigates'. Other ships in the Navy weren't rated but were still valuable because of their speed. These were armed schooners (two-masted ships with fore-and-aft sails) and armed cutters (single-masted with two headsails).

Sea Salt

Throughout Britain's maritime history, one man's name has stood above all the others. He is almost synonymous with the Royal Navy, the day of his death is still remembered over 200 years later, his flagship attracts visitors from all over the world and his statue looks down on a huge square in London that's devoted to his greatest naval victory. Who else could he be but Horatio, Viscount Nelson.

The man who became such a towering British hero was born in Burnham Thorpe in Norfolk on 29 September 1758. His father was the village rector, and Horatio was the sixth of eleven children. He was a delicate child and his world fell apart when he was ten with the death of his mother, Catherine. Catherine's brother, Captain Matthew Suckling, took the shattered boy under his wing and introduced him to life in the Royal Navy.

It was a brilliant move. At the precociously early age of 20, Nelson became a captain, and saw action in Britain's war with the American colonists. Yellow fever damaged his health for a time, and soon after his career went through a five-year fallow period with no work because he had upset the Admiralty by enforcing laws that other captains preferred to ignore out of self-interest. But at least it gave him time to get married to Frances 'Fanny' Nisbet. Everything changed in January 1793, when the French executed their king, Louis XVI. It was the start of a long period of warfare with the French, who were in a state of turbulent and bloody revolution, and it was also the making of Nelson's reputation as a great naval commander.

Many sea battles followed, and with them came the honours – and the injuries. He was virtually blinded in his right eye at the Battle of Calvi in Corsica in July 1794. The Battle of Cape St Vincent in 1797 won him a knighthood, but shortly after, during the Battle of Santa Cruz de Tenerife, his right elbow was shattered by grapeshot and the only recourse was amputation. After recuperating in England, he was back at sea in 1798 and scored a glorious triumph at the Battle of the Nile, when the French fleet was comprehensively defeated. A barony followed, making him Baron Nelson of the Nile. This disappointed him (it's the lowest order of the British nobility), and he said he would have preferred no title at all. King Ferdinand IV of Naples bestowed his own decoration on Nelson, giving him the dukedom of Bronte in Sicily, much to the outrage of the British Admiralty. But the British people had taken Nelson to their hearts as their hero, as he discovered when he arrived home in 1800. With him came Sir William Hamilton, the British diplomat who lived in Naples, and his wife Emma, who by now was having a red-hot affair with Nelson and who bore him a daughter, Horatia, in January 1801. Much to the outrage of many people, Nelson left his wife for Emma and lived quite openly with the Hamiltons. Sir William (who died in 1803) tolerated the situation, partly because he so admired Nelson.

Nelson scored another massive victory in April 1801 at the Battle of Copenhagen against the Dutch, when he ignored the signal to withdraw from the Fleet Commander. He put his telescope to his blind eye and told his Flag Lieutenant, 'You know, Foley, I have only one eye. I have a right to be blind sometimes. I really do not see the signal.' He then proceeded to pulverise the Dutch ships. Despite his defiance of orders, at long last Nelson became commander-in-chief of the Navy and was made a viscount.

Renewed hostilities broke out between Britain and France in early 1803 and Nelson was back in action, this time commanding the Navy's flagship, HMS *Victory*, in the Mediterranean. On 20 October 1805, the combined French and Spanish fleets were sighted and the British fleet prepared to do battle. In the early hours of the following morning, Nelson wrote his will and sent out the now famous signal to the rest of the Navy: 'England expects that every man will do his duty.'

The *Victory* came under heavy fire, and her captain, Thomas Hardy, suggested that Nelson remove the naval decorations on his coat because they made him an easy target of the enemy's snipers. But Nelson told him it was 'too late to be shifting a coat'. As men fell all around them, he commented 'this is too warm work to last long'. Even so, Nelson and Hardy continued to walk about the deck, giving orders to the men.

Suddenly, Hardy noticed that Nelson wasn't with him any longer. He had been hit by a sniper from the French ship *Redoubtable*, and told Hardy, 'I do believe they have done it at last ... my backbone is shot through.' He was carried below decks, on the way giving advice to a midshipman. Then he covered his face with a handkerchief so his men wouldn't know that he'd been fatally injured. He died later that afternoon, and his last words are reputed to have been, 'God and my country'.

Britain won the Battle of Trafalgar but lost a great hero. Nelson's body was put in a barrel of brandy that was lashed to the *Victory*'s mainmast and permanently guarded. News of the great victory, and Nelson's death, was rushed back to England by HMS *Pickle*, a schooner that had been at the battle although she was too small to take part in the action. The nation was devastated. Emma Hamilton collapsed on hearing the news. George III apparently said, 'We have lost more than we gained'. Nelson was given a state funeral on 9 January 1806 at St Paul's Cathedral in London, and his body placed in a magnificent black sarcophagus that had originally been made in the 16th century for Cardinal Wolsey before he so drastically fell out of favour with Henry VIII.

Nelson was said to be a vain man who took pride in his many accomplishments, so we can only surmise that he would have been thrilled to read the inscription on his coffin:

> The Most Noble Lord Horatio Nelson, Viscount and Baron
> Nelson, of the Nile and of Burnham Thorpe in the County
> of Norfolk, Baron Nelson of the Nile and of Hilborough
> in the said County, Knight of the Most Honourable Order of
> the Bath, Vice Admiral of the White Squadron of the
> Fleet, Commander in Chief of His Majesty's Ships and
> Vessels in the Mediterranean, Duke of Bronte in Sicily,
> Knight Grand Cross of the Sicilian Order of St Ferdinand
> and of Merit, Member of the Ottoman Order of the
> Crescent, Knight Grand Commander of the Order of St
> Joachim.

History has served him well but his mistress, Emma Hamilton, died destitute and forgotten in 1815. Nelson's instructions to the government to take care of her and their daughter Horatia were ignored. Horatia married the Rev. Philip Ward, who was then the curate at her father's village of Burnham Thorpe and went on to be a vicar in Norfolk and later in Tenterden in Kent. She originally called herself Nelson's adopted daughter, only later admitting that he really was her father. But she always distanced herself from the controversial figure of Emma Hamilton.

TIME FOR THE TOAST

The Navy has a different drinking toast for every day of the week. Traditionally, the toast is given by the newest midshipman or officer, and if he fails to remember what he's supposed to say he has to buy a round of drinks for everyone present.

These toasts follow the loyal toast (a toast to the reigning sovereign). The words in brackets are not said by the person giving the toast, but are often given as a response by everyone else.

Sunday	Absent friends
Monday	Our ships at sea
Tuesday	Our men
Wednesday	Ourselves (as no one else is likely to concern themselves with our welfare)
Thursday	A bloody war or a sickly season
Friday	A willing foe and sea room
Saturday	Sweethearts and wives (may they never meet)

JOIN THE WRENS AND FREE A MAN FOR THE FLEET

Before the early 20th century, women were only tolerated onboard ships, and their presence was restricted to providing what might be politely called home comforts. They certainly weren't allowed to serve as colleagues to the men.

But all that changed in November 1917, when the First World War was raging. The Women's Royal Naval Service (WRNS, also officially known as the Wrens) was formed. Its members worked as clerks, cooks, wireless telegraphists, air mechanics and electricians – all jobs that would normally be performed by men, who could therefore go off to fight. At first, the jobs were deliberately confined to the sort of tasks that were thought suitable to the so-called fairer sex, and therefore not very challenging. But the women proved they were capable of tackling much tougher jobs than had first been assigned to them. At their peak, there were 5,500 women in the WRNS. Their motto was 'Never at Sea'. The WRNS was disbanded in October 1919, after the war had ended.

Many people doubtless thought that was the end of that and a jolly good thing too, but the WRNS were revived in the months leading up to the Second World War. The plans were set in motion in 1938 when it became clear which way the wind was blowing on the world stage, and the WRNS was reformed in 1939 with the slogan, 'Join the Wrens and Free a Man for the Fleet'. It was a very select service at first and was considered to be the sole province of middle- and upper-class girls. The WRNS were widely considered to be the most glamorous of the women's services, and many of the Wrens admitted that they'd volunteered because of the flattering uniform.

The list of criteria for being eligible to join was initially quite strict (they included good qualifications in German, being related to someone in the Royal Navy or Merchant Navy, and practical experience of boat work) but the rules were relaxed as the war progressed and more women were needed. In addition to the jobs they'd performed in the First World War, they added exciting new tasks, including being meteorologists, radio operators, bomb range markers, cipher officers and coders. Many of them served abroad, often in very dangerous locations, but those who served in Britain were also in danger as they worked in ports that were frequently heavily bombed by German planes. They all had to use naval language, even if they always worked on dry land, so leaving their naval establishment (whose name was always prefaced by HMS) was referred to as 'going ashore', even if they only walked out of the gates. In 1944 there were 74,000 Wrens performing 200 different jobs.

They worked hard, but many of them also had a terrific time and made friendships that lasted for the rest of their lives. There were lots of jokes about them, too, which they mostly took in good part. One common naval saying was 'Up with the lark, to bed with the Wren' – something which must have alarmed a lot of naval wives. It is also alleged that when stocks of cloth were running low a signal was sent out to all the tailors who were contracted to the naval service, saying, 'Wren skirts will be held up until the ratings' needs are satisfied'.

By the end of the war the work of the WRNS had been so valuable that a permanent, but smaller, service of 3,000 women was established in February 1949, mainly in supportive and administrative roles at Royal Navy establishments both in the United Kingdom and abroad. In 1977 the WRNS became subject to the Naval Discipline Act, which broadened the scope of the work they could do and also put them on the same standing as their colleagues in the Air Force and the Army. The first women served onboard ship in 1990 and, as this didn't lead to the sexual mayhem that some doommongers had foretold (and some naval wives had feared), the WRNS was disbanded in 1993 and the women were fully incorporated into the Royal Navy. Today, about 3,700 women currently serve in the Royal Navy, making up about 10 per cent of naval personnel. Their WRNS predecessors would be proud of them.

FOR THOSE IN PERIL ON THE SEA

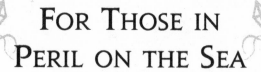

Dear Lord, be good to me
The sea is so wide
And my boat is so small.

IRISH FISHERMAN'S PRAYER

HEART OF OAK

Before the introduction of new ship designs, all English ships were built from wood. This was a very skilled business and every stage of the very long process involved care, forethought and tremendous knowledge. The best wood of all came from the English oak (*Quercus robur*), although other trees were used as well.

Oaks are slow-growing trees, so anyone who planted a tiny acorn would never live to see it grow into a huge tree that was ready to be felled. It was an activity that people undertook for the benefit of future generations, just as they were benefitting from the actions of their predecessors. Every step in the process was carefully considered and the trees were planted in specific groups according to their final purpose. Trees intended to make straight planks such as those used for ship decks were planted tightly together so they would all grow straight upwards in search of light. Trees needed for curved sections, such the hull, were spaced further apart in hedgerows. When the acorns fell each autumn, they were ideal food for the local pigs.

It was the perfect system. But there was a major snag. In the early Middle Ages, oak was being cut down in tremendous quantities to provide enough wood to build a ship, but for a long time not many people were thinking about replenishing the stocks by planting new forests. It was as though they imagined the supply would be endless.

But it wasn't. And with each year that passed when oaks weren't being planted in sufficient quantities, the legacy of a shortage of wood was being created.

One of the difficulties was the astonishing number of trees that went into making a single ship. In late Elizabethan times, about 2,000 mature oak trees, each about 100 years old, had to be felled to create a single warship. (According to a parliamentary report in 1812, the same number was needed to create a 74-gun warship.) In addition, extra trees were needed to provide green oak. This is 'wet' or unseasoned oak, which is more malleable and shrinks as it dries – ideal for creating completely watertight joints. And wood wasn't only used to make new ships – a huge number of trees went into repairing each of the existing ships whenever that became necessary.

By the time of Charles II in the 16th century, when Britain was recovering from the terrible effects of the Civil War, there was a severe shortage of oak. The Great Fire of London that destroyed so many buildings in 1666 didn't help, because it was generally believed (quite wrongly) that oak was the only wood that could resist fire, so it was chosen for much of the rebuilding of the city. There was another reason for the shortage: oak was the best wood for creating the charcoal that would smelt iron.

In fact, iron eventually took over from oak in the shipbuilding industry in the late 19th century. Shipbuilders were no longer entirely dependent on wood for their construction, but making ships made from iron (and later steel) was a more expensive business. So it was a maritime version of swings and roundabouts.

PRESS GANGS

In times of war, getting drunk in taverns in seaside towns or lying by the harbour waiting for your hangover to wear off could be a dangerous business if you were a man. You might easily be hauled off to the Navy by the impress service, which was commonly known as the press gang. Once you'd sobered up, you would be given the choice of either signing on as a volunteer, or you could refuse and become a pressed man. In other words, there was no escaping your fate.

If you agreed to sign on as a volunteer you did so on the same terms as anyone who had signed up willingly: you received conduct money and two months' pay in advance, out of which you had to buy your clothes, hammock and other equipment. There was an added inducement that made many men take 'the king's shilling', as it was called: you would be protected from your creditors if your debts were less than £20. If you were a pressed man, on the other hand, you didn't get a penny.

Impressment was, unsurprisingly, highly unpopular so laws were passed about it at various stages, either introducing greater leniency or, when war threatened, reducing the exemptions. For instance, an Act of Parliament in 1703 restricted impressment to men below the age of 18. But in 1740, the age barrier was raised dramatically to 55. Some people were exempt – apprentices, for example. Foreigners were also exempt, unless they had worked on a British merchant vessel for more than two years (in which case they were highly prized because they literally knew the ropes) or had a British wife. Any man who couldn't legally be impressed carried a certificate, issued by the Admiralty and Trinity House, known as a 'protection'. He would show this whenever the press gang came calling. However, this piece of paper was worthless in times of national crisis, when every man was needed.

One of these times was in July 1666 when England was in the thick of a war against the Dutch. Samuel Pepys observed men being impressed at the Tower of London and vividly recorded the experience in his diary: 'But Lord, how some poor women did cry, and in my life never did see such natural expression of passion as I did here – in some women's bewailing themselves, and running to every parcel of men that were brought, one after another, to look for their husbands, and wept over every vessel that went off, thinking they might be there, and looking after the ship as far as ever they could by moonlight, that it grieved me to the heart to hear them.' It wasn't only romantic love that made these women so desperate – they would also have been wondering how they were going to cope financially.

Worse was to come during the Napoleonic Wars of 1803–15. As far as the press gangs were concerned, every man was fair game, even if he was comfortably ensconced in the apparent safely of his own home. This is what happened at Harwich in 1803: 'The Market house was to be their prison, where a lieutenant was station'd with a guard of Marines and before daylight next morning their prison was full of all denominations, from the Parish Priest to the farmer in his frock and wooden shoes. Even the poor Blacksmith cobbler taylor barber baker fisherman and doctor were all dragg'd from their homes that night…'

Although impressment wasn't used after 1815 the Navy kept the right to enforce it if necessary. This effectively ended in 1853 when the Navy introduced a fixed period of service for sailors, ending with a pension when they retired.

A different sort of impressment, one that also pressed young men into the Army and Air Force, was introduced in the 20th century. This was National Service, which only ended in the early 1960s.

Hard Tack and Weevils

Life onboard ship can be tough, but was especially so in previous centuries. Not only did you have to withstand the rigours of the weather, the danger of pirates, the threat of contagious diseases and the psychological difficulties of being cooped up with the same group of people for weeks if not months at a time, but you also had to stomach the food. Ideally, the cargo included plenty of live animals and a butcher-cum-cook to turn them into delicious grub. But the cook and his menagerie took up valuable space, and when the animals had all been eaten the ship had to sail into port to pick up the next batch of live supplies destined for the pot. How much easier to take food that could last for weeks, months or even years without it going off. Enter hard tack.

This is a thinnish biscuit made from flour, water and salt. It doesn't contain yeast, so it won't rise in the oven. It doesn't contain fat, so it won't turn rancid. And it is baked hard, so it will take some time to soften up. It was baked twice for normal voyages, but four times for long sea voyages to ensure its keeping qualities. Records indicate that it was sometimes still being handed out as rations 40 years after it had been baked. No wonder sailors (and soldiers, since it was also valuable in the army) nicknamed their biscuits 'tooth dullers' and 'sheet iron', among other less polite epithets.

One of the best ways to eat hard tack was to dunk it in whatever you were drinking, in the hope that this might make it edible. You had to get used to it because you often had to eat rather a lot of it: sailors in the Royal Navy in the late 16th century were given 1 pound (0.45 kg) of hard tack a day and 1 gallon (4.5 litres) of beer. Hard tack only disappeared from the Navy's menu in the mid-1800s when canned foods were introduced: tins of preserved beef officially became part of the rations in 1847. Luckily for sailors, it also became possible to bake bread onboard ship in the mid-1850s, so they were able to eat wheat in a more palatable form than before. This bread was known as 'soft tack'.

It was essential to store the hard tack properly. Sailors might have found it tough to eat but insects weren't so choosy. They would happily eat their way into it, especially weevils, many of which are particularly drawn to farinaceous products. One way to get rid of them was to tap the biscuit sharply on a hard surface. The weevils would fall out, and you could chew the hard tack in peace.

THE SCOURGE OF SCURVY

From the end of the 15th century until the late 18th century, sailors had to face a terrible enemy that came from their own side. It could be considered an early form of 'friendly fire' and it decimated the crews of ships on long voyages. It was scurvy.

This deadly disease laid waste to sailors who were afflicted with the most gruesome symptoms that included swollen gums, loose teeth, foul-smelling breath, respiratory difficulties, extreme fatigue, personality disorders, extreme emotions and, eventually, death. Sailors knew what the problem was, but no one knew what caused it. There were all sorts of theories, from foul air to melancholia, as well as speculation that perhaps it was connected with the amount of salt that sailors consumed while being at sea for months on end, as their main food was preserved meat. Sailors often recovered almost miraculously quickly when they made landfall and started eating local plants, so they thought their cure might have something to do with them being on dry land again.

What no one realised for centuries was that the fault lay solely in the highly restricted diet of salted meat, beer and hard tack that the sailors ate. It was deficient in vitamins, especially B and C, and the problem was compounded if sailors ate the livers of passing seals as these gave them a dangerous overdose of vitamin A.

Eventually, the penny began to drop that the cause of scurvy revolved around diet, and in 1753 the Scottish physician James Lind published his *Treatise of the Scurvy*, which claimed that fresh vegetables and citrus fruits were the only cure. The ships' rations were enriched with various foodstuffs, including malt, vinegar, mustard, beans, portable soup made from dried vegetables, and rob, which was a concentrated fruit juice. Unfortunately, rob was no good whatsoever because it lost all its vitamin C content during its production, not that anyone knew that at the time. The long Pacific voyages undertaken by British ships in the 1760s were intended to experiment with the sailors' diets and keep scurvy at bay. Captain James Cook, who was one of the officers involved in the experiment, was convinced that regular doses of malt were the answer. They weren't.

In 1794 Rear Admiral Alan Gardner and other senior officers insisted that lemon juice was issued to the men onboard HMS *Suffolk* during a six-month voyage to India. The sailors only received a tiny amount each day but it was enough to keep scurvy at bay. Although the Navy soon accepted the notion that lemon juice should be issued to all sailors, this couldn't be done because it was in such short supply. This situation only changed after 1800.

As for the recognition of the existence of vitamin C, that didn't happen until 1932. At long last, the medical profession was able to confirm that lack of the vitamin led to scurvy. What Captain Cook would have said about that is anyone's guess.

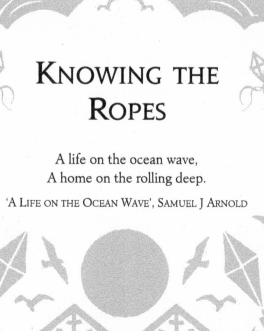

KNOWING THE ROPES

A life on the ocean wave,
A home on the rolling deep.

'A LIFE ON THE OCEAN WAVE', SAMUEL J ARNOLD

SALTY SPEECH

As Britain is a seafaring nation, the British language is awash with phrases that originated onboard ship, even though these phrases are now used by landlubbers who have no idea of where they come from. Here is a selection of some of the most interesting ones.

LETTING THE CAT OUT OF THE BAG This metaphor for divulging a secret has nothing to do with sweet little Tiddles being released from captivity. It refers to the production of the cat o' nine tails – a whip that consisted of nine separate lashes, each one bearing a knot – before a sailor was punished by being hit on the bare back with it. The cat was kept in a bag made from red baize, and production of it was doubtless something to be dreaded.

NO ROOM TO SWING A CAT This phrase conjures up unpleasant images of our friend Tiddles being grasped by his tail as someone tries to whirl him around their head. In fact, it refers to the period when sailors were punished by being flogged with a cat o' nine tails. This usually took place in the small area between the poop and the main-mast, so it was difficult to administer the punishment without hitting something – or someone – by accident.

SHOW A LEG Today we say this when we are urging someone to get on with things pretty sharpish. But it dates from the days until about 1840 when women were allowed to sleep onboard ship while it was in harbour. The fear was that if men were granted shore leave they might not return to their ships, so the women were allowed to come to them instead. Every morning, after the sailors got up, the boatswain would check each hammock for malingerers. Any occupant had to put their leg over the edge of the hammock, and that would be the clue as to whether it was a woman or a sailor hoping for a lie-in.

SON OF A GUN Today, this expression is used to express aston-ishment and also approval. In the past, sailors used it to express contempt for one another, because of the origin of the phrase. When women were allowed to live onboard ship it wasn't unusual for them to give birth there. The only place for them to do this was on the gun deck. However, this had to be kept clear at all times in case of enemy action, so the women would give birth in the spaces between the guns. Very often a woman wasn't sure who was the father of her child, so if she gave birth to a boy he would be entered in the ship's log as a 'son of a gun'. In other words, his father was unknown.

SWEET FANNY ADAMS Nowadays, this phrase (sometimes short-ened to 'sweet FA') describes something that's useless. It sounds quite harmless but it has a gruesome origin that coincides with the intro-duction of tinned meat into naval rations. In 1867 a young girl called Fanny Adams was murdered and dismembered. Sailors joked that her body had been turned into their rations. The 'sweet' part of the saying refers to the child's innocence.

TAKING THE GILT OFF THE GINGERBREAD Today, this means allowing harsh reality to intrude on an illusion. It originates from the time when the bow and stern of warships were decorated with beautiful gilded carvings, known as gingerbread after the orna-mental gingerbread cakes that were so popular at the time. When either the carvings or their decoration was damaged, thereby annoying the captain, sailors would say the gilt was taken off the gingerbread.

THE DEVIL TO PAY Today, this means having to shoulder a very difficult punishment. When it originated, it was essential to keep all the seams of a ship's side watertight, and this was done by 'paying' each one with oakum and covering it with hot pitch. The trickiest seam of the lot was the one nearest the ship's bulwark, so it was called 'the devil'. From this, we also get 'between the devil and the deep blue sea', because any sailor attending to this seam was in danger of toppling over the side of the ship.

TO KNOW THE ROPES This now means feeling familiar with a particular procedure. It stems from the importance of sailors knowing which rope to use at any given moment.

AT THE RATE OF KNOTS

Speed, distance and depth are measured differently when dealing with water rather than on dry land. Distance at sea is measured in nautical miles, with one nautical mile being equal to one minute of arc of latitude (the imaginary lines that run from west to east around the Earth). This distance is slightly increased near the North and South poles, where the Earth flattens out. How long is a nautical mile? It's approximately 1.15 statute (land) miles (or 1.852 km).

Speed at sea is measured in knots, with one knot equalling one nautical mile. Originally, the speed of a ship was measured using real knots. An object known as a chip log, which looked like a slice of pie and had a lead weight attached to its curved side, was connected to a long line of rope in which knots were tied at regular intervals of approximately 47 feet (14.3 metres). The chip log was thrown overboard and would float upright, creating resistance in the water. One sailor would put his hands around the line, counting the number of knots that passed through his fingers in 30 seconds, while another sailor would hold a sandglass to measure the exact time. The number of knots that passed through the sailor's hands represented the rate of knots at which the ship was moving. This is where we get the phrase 'at the rate of knots', which means moving at high speed.

Depth at sea is measured in fathoms. Many measurements were originally based on the length of various parts of the body (for instance, originally distance was paced out by foot, which is how we get the imperial measurement of a foot). A fathom is the longest of these anatomical units of measurement, and was originally the distance of a man's fully extended arms when measured from the outstretched middle finger of one hand to the outstretched middle finger of the other. (Interestingly, this distance is equal to that person's height.) 'Fathom' comes from the Old English *faedm*, meaning 'outstretched arms'. Today the fathom has been standardised for several countries, including the UK and the US, at 6 feet (1.8288 metres).

WHEN EIGHT BELLS TOLL

For centuries, time was marked onboard ship with the tolling of a bell. But it didn't sound the hours in the manner of a normal clock. Instead, it marked the passing of each watch (or shift) onboard ship, so sailors knew when they were on duty.

Each watch lasted for four hours, and the passing of each half-hour within that watch was marked by a toll of the bell. It was a very simple system because each successive half-hour meant an extra toll of the bell. Half-hours had an odd number of tolls, while full hours were marked by an even number. So the first half hour ('one bell') had one toll; the first hour ('two bells') was marked by two tolls rung as a pair;

an hour and a half ('three bells') was marked by three tolls, rung as a pair followed by a single toll, and so on. 'Eight bells', which was rung as four pairs of two tolls, meant that four hours had passed, so it was the end of duty for one watch and the start of duty for the next. In nautical parlance, 'eight bells' means 'finish'.

On New Year's Eve, the arrival of midnight was marked by sixteen bells – eight bells for the old year and eight for the new one.

How did the sailors know when to toll the bell? The half-hours were measured using a 30-minute sandglass. Whenever the final dribbles of sand ran through from the top of the sandglass to the bottom, the bell would be tolled. Some sailors had a clever dodge of hurrying up the end of their watches. They would warm the neck of the sandglass in the hope that this would make the glass expand so the sand would pass through the sandglass more quickly. This was known as 'warming the bell', even though the bell itself wasn't warmed.

THE SHIP'S BELL

Even today, when so many tasks onboard ship are automated, the ship's bell still has a vital role to play. So much so, in fact, that maritime law dictates that every ship should carry a sound bell. This is for safety reasons, because a ship's bell is rung repeatedly whenever the ship encounters foggy weather, so as to alert any other ships or small craft that might be in the vicinity. The bell is also rung if fire breaks out onboard.

The bell also comes into its own under the much happier circumstance of a child being baptised onboard ship. The bell is inverted and filled with holy water, so it can act as a font. The child's name is then inscribed on the inside of the bell.

Tradition dictates that the ship's name should be engraved on her bell, which is made of brass, sometimes with her year of launching as well. Some bells also carry the name of the shipyard in which the ship was built. There is a practical purpose to this, because if the ship is wrecked the bell may be an important clue to her identity and origin.

During maritime battles, capturing the bell of an enemy's ship was considered to be a great prize because it proved that the ship could no longer function.

PORT AND STARBOARD

Do you know your port from your starboard, or your aft from your stern? Nautical terms are a language all of their own. Here are some of them.

Adrift	Something that is afloat and not attached to any kind of mooring, yet which is not under way
Aft	Near or towards the stern of a ship
Aground	When a ship's bottom is resting on the seabed, as in 'running aground'
Ahoy	A cry to draw attention
All hands	Everyone onboard ship
Aloft	High above the ship's solid structure, such as in the rigging
Anchorage	A suitable place to weigh anchor
Articles of War	The regulations governing the Royal Navy
Bar pilot	Someone who guides ships over treacherous sandbars in bays and rivers

Beam	The width of a vessel at her widest point (from which we get the phrase 'broad in the beam')
Bight	A loop tied in a rope or line. Also an indentation in the coastline
Bitter end	The last part of a rope or cable
Block	A single pulley or a set of pulleys
Blue Peter	A blue and white flag (originally a white ship on a blue background, now a white square on a blue background) that is hoisted before a ship sails
Boom	A spar run out to extend the bottom of a sail
Bosun	The popular name for the boatswain (pronounced *bos'n*) – a ship's officer who is responsible for the equipment and the crew
Bow	The forward part of the ship from the point at which her sides begin to curve inwards until they meet at the stem
Bowsprit	A spar extending from the bow that acts as an anchor for the forestay and rigging
Bulwark	The solid part of the ship's side extending above the level of the deck
Cable	A large rope
CQD	The original radio distress call made by a ship needing assistance. It was introduced in 1904 and superseded in 1908 by 'SOS'. 'CQ' was a sign for 'all stations' and 'D' meant 'distress'. It was popularly known as 'Come Quickly, Danger'
Civil Red Ensign	The ensign of the British Merchant Navy. It is a red flag with the Union Flag in the top left quarter. Affectionately called 'the red duster'
Cockpit	The area, housing the rudder controls, towards the stern of a small ship. Originally it was the compartment beneath the gun deck of a man-of-war where the wounded were taken during battle
Corsair	A privateer, especially from the Barbary Coast of North Africa. Also the name given to their very fast ships

Coxswain	Pronounced *coxs'n*. The crew member in charge of the boat and the rest of the crew
Dead ahead	Exactly ahead
Drink	Old Navy slang for being in the sea, as in 'he landed in the drink'
Flagship	The ship of the fleet that carries the commanding admiral
Flotsam	Cargo or debris that floats on the sea or into shore after a shipwreck
Fo'c'stle	The forecastle, or the area before the mast; traditionally the sailors' living quarters
Forestays	Long lines or cables that support the mast, running from the bow to the mastheads
Galley	The kitchen area of a ship
Grapeshot	Small balls of lead shot fired from a cannon
Grog	Alcohol, traditionally rum and water
Gunwale	Pronounced *gunn'l*. The upper edge of the hull
Halyard	The rope used to raise or lower the head of a sail
Hammock	The canvas sheet slung from hooks in the deck beams, in which sailors slept. Hammocks were first officially issued in the Navy in 1597
Hand	A member of the ship's crew
Helmsman	The person steering the vessel
Jetsam	Goods or other material that has been thrown overboard, especially to lighten the ship's load, and washed ashore
Lee side	The side of the vessel sheltered from the wind
List	The vessel's tilt to one side, in the direction known as 'roll'
Mainmast	The tallest mast on the ship
Man-of-war	Warship from the age of sailing ships
Mayday	The international radio-telephonic (therefore verbal) distress signal used by ships and aircraft. It is the phonetic spelling of the French *m'aidez*, or 'help me'
Mess	Where the sailors eat

Poop deck	The highest deck on the aft of a ship
Port	The side of the ship to your left when the ship is facing forward. It's denoted at night by a red light. It was previously called 'larboard'
Privateer	Privately owned ship commissioned by a country or national power to carry out hostile acts against the enemy
Quarterboard	The raised section of the deck that runs from the mainmast to the stern
Rigging	The masts and lines (ropes) on a ship
Roll	A ship's side-to-side motion in the water
Sextant	Navigational instrument to measure a ship's latitude
Shoal	An area of shallow water that is a navigational hazard
Shroud	A rope that prevents the sideways movement of a mast
Skipper	The ship's captain
SOS	The internationally agreed distress call transmitted in Morse Code by a ship in distress. It was adopted worldwide in 1908 and the letters were chosen because they are easy to transmit and understand in Morse Code: three dots, three dashes, three dots
Spar	A strong, thick pole
Splice	To join two lines (ropes) by unravelling their ends and entwining them
Starboard	The side of the ship to your right when the ship is facing forward. It's denoted at night by a green light
Stay	Part of the rigging that supports a mast in the fore-and-aft position
Stern	The rear of a ship
Topsail	The second sail up from the bottom of a mast
Under way	A vessel that is moving under control
Wake	The choppy waters immediately behind a vessel
Wash	The waves created as a vessel moves through the water
White Ensign	The flag flown on Royal Navy ships. It is a white flag bearing a thin cross of St George, with the Union

	Flag in the top left quarter. Also known as St George's Ensign
Windward	The direction from which the wind is blowing; facing the wind
Yard	A horizontal spar from which a sail hangs on a ship's mast
Yardarm	Each end of the yard of a square-rigged ship

AND NOW THE SHIPPING FORECAST

Four times each day, you can hear a detailed forecast on BBC Radio of the weather for all the shipping areas around the United Kingdom and beyond, stretching up to the waters around Iceland and down to the sea bordering the northern coast of Spain. The Shipping Forecast, as it's called, has an indefinable quality that attracts many listeners, and not only those who are afloat. Many committed land-lubbers who would never dream of setting foot on a boat also tune in, lulled by the magic of the words and the romance of all those names. We tend to take the Shipping Forecast for granted, especially in these days of satellite navigation, but when it was first developed it was intended to save many lives. And it did.

We have one man to thank for the development of the Shipping Forecast. He was Captain (later Vice Admiral) Robert FitzRoy RN, who was born in 1805 into an aristocratic English family whose ancestors included Charles II. He made a name for himself at least three times over: he was the Governor of New Zealand; he worked to save countless lives on the seas and also become the founder of the Met

Office; and he was the captain of HMS *Beagle* on her five-year voyage of surveillance around South America when a certain Charles Darwin was an essential member of the crew. Another member of the crew was Francis Beaufort, a hydrographer who later developed his Beaufort Scale for measuring wind speed at sea.

After returning to Britain following the difficult task of being the second Governor of New Zealand (something of a poisoned chalice), FitzRoy was given a new challenge – to improve safety at sea by distributing information about the meteorological conditions. An international conference in 1853 had discussed the need for meteorological information at sea because so many lives were being lost. In 1854 FitzRoy was made head of a new department and given the grand title of Meteorological Statist to the Board of Trade. This was the beginning of what we know as the Met Office. FitzRoy asked naval captains to supply him with plenty of information, including temperature, wind speed and humidity, and he compiled his own charts from the data he received. He also invented two types of barometer to measure atmospheric conditions.

In the late summer of 1859, more than 200 ships were wrecked around the coast of Britain in a mere two weeks. As a result, FitzRoy was inspired to set up 15 weather stations around the British coast, all of which telegraphed their data to London. He used this information to create synoptic charts, which are still in use today, and his forecasts of the weather (from which we get the term 'weather forecasts') were first published daily in *The Times*. Sadly, FitzRoy did not share history's estimation of his abilities and committed suicide in 1865.

The first Shipping Forecast was broadcast to British shipping on the new-fangled wireless on 1 January 1924. It was called 'Weather Shipping' and was sent out twice a day from the Air Ministry in London. It went off the air during the Second World War but returned when peace was restored, and in 1949 it was expanded into the form we know today.

The Shipping Forecast follows a strict format, beginning with any warnings of gales. These are followed by the General Synopsis, which always takes the same route through the 31 shipping areas, starting with Viking and ending with South-East Iceland. Only the 0048 GMT broadcast includes Trafalgar. Although the Shipping Forecast sounds highly complicated to uninitiated ears, it only gives three pieces of information for each region.

The wind speed and direction	For instance, 'south-easterly, veering southerly 4 or 5'
The weather	For instance, 'occasional rain or showers'
The visibility	For instance, 'moderate or good'

WHO, WHAT AND WHERE?

If you have ever listened to the Shipping Forecast (something that is strangely soothing, especially if you're warm and dry at home), you will have noticed the curious names of some of the 31 sea areas into which the British waters are currently divided. How did these areas get their names, what do they mean and where are they? Their precise map co-ordinates are given at the end of each entry.

VIKING This is the stretch of sea between Fair Isle and North Utsire, which lies off the coast of Norway.

61°00'N   00°00'W
61°00'N   04°00'E
58°30'N   04°00'E
58°30'N   00°00'W

NORTH UTSIRE This sea area borders the Norwegian coast. It gets its name from the island of Utsira. This sea area was introduced in 1984, before which it was part of Viking.

61°00'N   04°00'E
61°00'N   05°00'E
59°00'N   05°35'E
59°00'N   04°00'E

SOUTH UTSIRE This sea area lies below North Utsire on the Norwegian coast. It was introduced in 1984, before which it was part of Viking. The sea area of Fisher lies south of it, with Forties and Viking to the west.

59°00'N   04°00'E
59°00'N   05°35'E
57°45'N   07°30'E
57°45'N   04°00'E

FORTIES This area lies between South Utsire to the east and Cromarty and Forth to the west. It's situated in the area of the North Sea known as the Long Forties because it has a fairly consistent depth of 40 fathoms (73 metres).

58°30'N   01°00'W
58°30'N   04°00'E
56°00'N   04°00'E
56°00'N   01°00'W

CROMARTY The sea area of Cromarty lies off the far north-east coast of Scotland, with Fair Isle to the north, Forties to the east and Forth to the south. It gets its name from the former county of Cromartyshire. In Gaelic, Cromarty means 'crooked bay'.

57°00'N   02°10'W
57°00'N   01°00'W
58°30'N   01°00'W
58°30'N   03°00'W

FORTH This sea area lies off the north-east coast of Scotland and gets its name from the mouth of the River Forth. Cromarty lies to the north, Forties to the east and Tyne to the south.

55°40'N   01°50'W
56°00'N   01°00'W
57°00'N   01°00'W
57°00'N   02°10'W

TYNE Tyne lies off the coast of north-east England, and is named after the mighty River Tyne. Forth is to the north, Dogger to the east and Humber to the south.

54°15'N   00°20'W
54°15'N   00°45'W
56°00'N   01°00'W
55°40'N   01°50'W

DOGGER This gets its name from the large sandbank, known as Dogger Bank, that lies in the North Sea between north-east England and north-west Denmark. The name Dogger is derived from *dogge*, which is an Old Dutch word for fishing boat. Forties lies to the north, German Byte to the east, Humber to the south and Tyne to the west.

57°00'N   02°30'E
56°00'N   01°00'W
54°15'N   00°45'E
54°15'N   04°00'E
56°00'N   04°00'E

FISHER Like Dogger, this area is named after a sandbank. In this case, it is Fisher Bank. Fisher lies off the west coast of Denmark, with South Utsire to the north, German Bight to the south and Forties to the west. It was introduced as a sea area in 1955.

57°45'N   04°00'E
56°00'N   04°00'E
56°00'N   08°10'E
57°05'N   08°35'E
57°45'N   07°30'E

GERMAN BIGHT A bight is a wide bay, and German Bight is the huge area of water that lies off the northern Netherlands and western Denmark (with Germany sandwiched between them) and contains the Frisian and Danish Islands. German Bight was called Heligoland

in UK Shipping Forecasts between 1949 and 1956. Fisher lies to the
north, with Dogger and Humber to the west.

56°00'N   08°10'E
56°00'N   04°00'E
54°15'N   04°00'E
53°35'N   04°40'E
52°45'N   04°40'E

HUMBER This gets its name from the Humber estuary which it
encompasses. It has Tyne and Dogger to the north, German Bight to
the east and Thames to the south.

52°45'N   01°40'E
52°45'N   04°40'E
53°35'N   04°40'E
54°15'N   04°00'E
54°15'N   00°20'W

THAMES Here is another sea area that gets its name from a huge estuary.
Thames lies between eastern England and the Belgian and Dutch coastlines. It has Humber to the north and Dover to the south-east.

51°15'N   01°25'E
51°15'N   02°55'E
52°45'N   04°40'E
52°45'N   01°40'E

DOVER This is a small sea area that lies in the narrowest part of the
English Channel (the Strait of Dover), separating south-eastern
England and north-eastern France. Thames lies to the north and
Wight to the west.

50°45'N   00°15'E
50°15'N   01°30'E
51°15'N   02°55'E
51°15'N   01°25'E

WIGHT This area gets its name from the Isle of Wight, and stretches between southern England and northern France. It has Dover to the west and Portland to the east.

50°35'N   01°55'W
49°45'N   01°55'W
50°15'N   01°30'E
50°45'N   00°15'E

PORTLAND This area includes Portland Harbour, hence its name, and it lies between southern England and north-western France. It encompasses the Channel Islands. Wight lies to the east and Plymouth to the west.

50°25'N   03°30'W
48°50'N   03°30'W
49°45'N   01°55'W
50°35'N   01°55'W

PLYMOUTH Bordering the south-western tip of England and the northwestern tip of France, Plymouth stretches out into the Atlantic Ocean. Portland lies to the east, Biscay to the south, Sole to the west and Lundy to the north.

50°05'N   05°45'W
50°00'N   06°15'W
48°27'N   06°15'W
48°27'N   04°45'W
48°50'N   03°30'W
50°25'N   03°30'W

BISCAY This is a huge sea area that runs from north-western France down to northern Spain, and it gets its name from the Bay of Biscay. Plymouth lies to the north and FitzRoy to the west.

48°27'N   06°15'W
43°35'N   06°15'W
48°27'N   04°45'W

TRAFALGAR This is the southernmost sea area and lies off the coast of Portugal and southern Spain. It has FitzRoy to the north.

35°00'N   15°00'W
35°00'N   06°15'W
41°00'N   08°40'W
41°00'N   15°00'W

FITZROY Until 2002 this sea area was called Finistere, but it was renamed in honour of Vice Admiral Robert FitzRoy RN, who was the founder of what became the Met Office. It covers the north-western tip of Spain and reaches far out into the North Atlantic, with the sea area Sole to the north, Biscay to the east and Trafalgar to the south.

48°27'N   15°00'W
41°00'N   15°00'W
41°00'N   08°40'W
43°35'N   06°15'W
48°27'N   06°15'W

SOLE This gets its name from two sandbanks that lie within it: the Great Sole Bank and the Little Sole Bank. It has no land barrier and lies south-west of Cornwall, with Shannon and Fastnet to the north, Plymouth to the east and FitzRoy to the south.

50°00'N   06°15'W
50°00'N   15°00'W
48°27'N   15°00'W
48°27'N   06°15'W

LUNDY This is named after the island in the Bristol Channel and stretches between south-west England and the eastern coast of Ireland. Irish Sea lies to the north, Fastnet to the west and Plymouth to the south.

52°30'N   06°15'W
50°00'N   06°15'W
50°05'N   05°45'W
52°00'N   05°05'W

FASTNET This sea area gets its name from Fastnet Rock, which lies off the southern coast of Ireland. Fastnet is *Carraig Aonair* in Irish, meaning 'solitary rock'. Shannon lies to the west, Lundy to the east and Sole to the south.

51°35'N   10°00'W
50°00'N   10°00'W
50°00'N   06°15'W
52°30'N   06°15'W

IRISH SEA Unsurprisingly, this area includes the Irish Sea, lying between north-west England and the east coast of Ireland and south-east coast of Northern Ireland. It has Malin to the north and Lundy to the south.

54°50'N   05°05'W
54°45'N   05°45'W
52°30'N   06°15'W
52°00'N   05°05'W

SHANNON This sea area gets its name from the Shannon estuary and borders the west coast of Ireland. It has Rockall to the north and Sole to the south.

53°30'N   15°00'W
50°00'N   15°00'W
50°00'N   10°00'W
51°35'N   10°00'W
53°30'N   10°05'W

ROCKALL The small uninhabited islet of Rockall has given its name to this sea area, which has no land boundaries, in the North Atlantic Ocean. Bailey lies to the north, Hebrides and Malin to the east and Shannon to the south.

58°00'N   10°00'W
58°00'N   15°00'W

53°30'N   15°00'W
53°30'N   10°05'W
54°20'N   10°00'W

MALIN This gets its name from Malin Head on the Inishowen Peninsula in the north of Ireland. It borders the north coasts of Ireland and Northern Ireland to the south and north-west Scotland to the east.

57°00'N   05°50'W
57°00'N   10°00'W
54°20'N   10°00'W
54°45'N   05°45'W
54°50'N   05°05'W

HEBRIDES As its name suggests, this sea area encompasses the Hebrides in north-west Scotland as well as Scotland's north-westerly coast. Faroes lies to the north, Fair Isle to the east, Malin to the south, Rockall to the south-west and Bailey to the north-west.

60°35'N   10°00'W
57°00'N   10°00'W
57°00'N   05°50'W
58°40'N   05°00'W

BAILEY This sea area lies far out in the North Atlantic Ocean, midway between northern Scotland and southern Iceland. Its neighbours are South-East Iceland to the north, Faroes to the north-east, Hebrides to the south-east and Rockall to the south.

62°25'N   15°00'W
58°00'N   15°00'W
58°00'N   10°00'W
60°35'N   10°00'W

FAIR ISLE Fair Isle is named after the remote Scottish island of the same name. Faroes lies to the north-west, Viking to the east and Hebrides to the south.

61°50'N   02°30'W
59°30'N   07°15'W
58°40'N   05°00'W
58°30'N   03°00'W
58°30'N   00°00'W
61°00'N   00°00'W

FAEROES This sea area is named after the Faroe Islands, which lie at roughly the midpoint between Scotland, Iceland and Norway, even though they belong to Denmark. South-East Iceland lies to the north-west, Fair Isle to the south-east, Bailey to the south-west and Hebdrides to the south.

63°20'N   07°30'W
61°10'N   11°30'W
59°30'N   07°15'W
61°50'N   02°30'W

SOUTH-EAST ICELAND Its name is self-explanatory – it lies off the south-east coast of Iceland. It is the northernmost sea area in the UK. Faroes lies to the south-east and Bailey to the south.

63°35'N   18°00'W
61°10'N   11°30'W
63°20'N   07°30'W
65°00'N   13°35'W

GET KNOTTED!

One of the first things a sailor must learn is how to tie ropes securely so they won't unravel until they're needed. It would be a disaster if a boat drifted away from the quay because its rope had untied itself. In one of the many examples of nautical-speak, a rope is a rope when it's ashore but becomes a line when it's onboard ship, unless it's given a specific name such as a tack.

There are many different knots, each of which performs a specific function, but here is a selection. Some of them belong to the same family of knots. Bends are used to secure one rope to another; hitches are used to tie a rope to an object; single-loop knots are used when throwing a rope over something; double-loop knots are more secure than single-loop knots but perform the same function.

Anchor bend	The knot used to fasten a line to an anchor
Bowline	A secure knot
Bowline on a bight	A loop in the middle of a line
Buntline hitch	The knot used to tie something to the end of a rope
Carrick bend	The knot that joins two heavy ropes together
Cleat hitch	The knot that ties a rope to a cleat
Clove hitch	A simple knot for tying a rope to a post
Figure-eight	The strongest knot for a loop at the end of a rope
Half-hitch	A basic knot often used in a supporting role; two half-hitches can tie a rope to an object

Heaving line knot	This adds weight to the end of a rope, making it easier to handle
Midshipman's hitch	An adjustable and secure knot, also called the tautline hitch
Mooring hitch	A knot that quickly releases
Monkey's fist	A decorative ball that takes practice to get right
Rolling bend	Used to secure a line to a post
Rolling hitch	Used to tie a line to a post; more secure than a clove hitch
Running bowline	A way of tying a slip knot to make an adjustable loop
Sheepshank	Used to shorten a rope; not a stable knot
Sheet bend	A knot used to join two ropes of different sizes
Slip knot	A knot used for a sliding loop
Slipped buntline	A knot that's quickly released with a pull on the tag end
Square knot	Once used to secure things onboard ship and for reefing sails; also known as a reef knot

TAKE THAT!

It has always been essential to keep order onboard ship, not only so it will function as efficiently as possible in what can be dangerous conditions but also to quell any hint of insurrection that might lead to a mutiny. In days gone by, all punishments were administered on deck in front of the rest of the crew, so they could see what lay in store for them if they committed a similar offence.

BIRCHING This was the Navy's standard method of corporal punishment from the 1860s, taking over from the cat o' nine tails. It involved hitting the sailor's bare buttocks (a humiliation in itself) with a switch of leafless twigs. It could be extremely painful, depending on the type of wood used for the twigs. Apparently hazel twigs were especially vicious.

CAT O' NINE TAILS Until the 1860s, sailors were flogged on the bare back with 'the cat', as it was called – a whip made from nine cords lashed together. The cords were knotted, to inflict greater pain. Naval regulations stipulated a maximum of 12 lashes during a punishment, but sailors often endured many more than this. The crime of theft (which was considered an outrage by men who had to trust one another because they lived in such close proximity) was punished with the thieves' cat, which had up to three knots in each cord. The cat was also known as 'the captain's daughter'.

FLOGGING This was the most common punishment onboard ship, whether with a cat o' nine tails or a birch rod.

FLOGGING ROUND THE FLEET This really let the punishment fit the crime. Very severe crimes, such as mutiny, might be punished by the entire fleet. Flogging round the fleet was a punishment that could take months if not years, as the malefactor was flogged on each ship in turn and his skin had to be allowed to heal before the next flogging.

KEELHAULING This was a severe punishment used on both naval and merchant ships in which ropes were tied around the miscreant's hands and feet, and he was then dragged under the ship's keel from one side to the other. If he tried to hasten the process he was quite likely to be cut to ribbons by the barnacles that covered the ship's hull. An even worse form of punishment was to be dragged beneath the ship from stem to stern. This usually ended in death, whether by drowning or from the injuries sustained during the punishment.

KISSING THE GUNNER'S DAUGHTER Don't be fooled by the attractive name of this punishment. It involved a sailor bending over the barrel of a gun, his bottom bared, in readiness for a harsh beating.

MAROONING Occasionally a sailor – or a captain if his men mutinied – would be punished by being left behind on a deserted island when the ship sailed. There was no means of escape. The man would be given some water, a little food and a loaded pistol in case he wanted to kill himself. Marooning was a particular favourite of pirates.

OVER A BARREL Before a sailor was flogged, he would be tied to a mast or a barrel to stop him escaping. This is where we get the phrase about someone having us 'over a barrel' when we're in a tight spot.

RUNNING THE GAUNTLET This was a punishment for theft that allowed the entire ship's crew to express their feelings towards the perpetrator. The crew would assemble in two rows and the thief would run between them while being lashed by each sailor with a short knotted rope known as a 'nettle'.

WALKING THE PLANK A sailor, sometimes with his hands or feet bound together, would be made to walk along a plank that jutted out over the side of the ship, ending in mid-air. He would fall off and be left to drown. It has often been thought that this punishment belongs solely to the world of fiction but there are historical records of sailors being made to walk the plank.

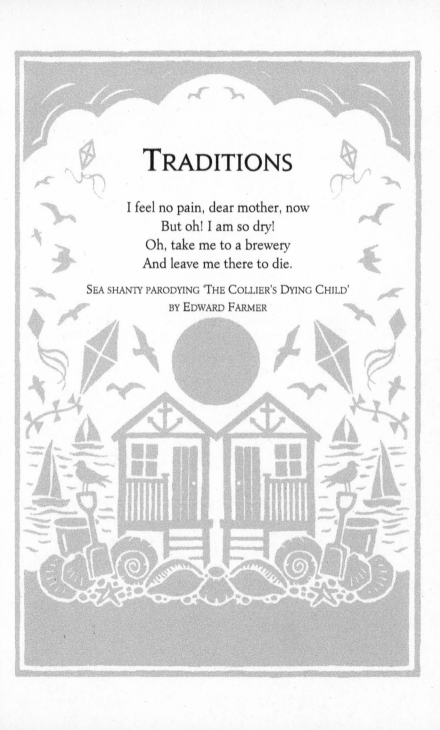

TRADITIONS

I feel no pain, dear mother, now
But oh! I am so dry!
Oh, take me to a brewery
And leave me there to die.

SEA SHANTY PARODYING 'THE COLLIER'S DYING CHILD'
BY EDWARD FARMER

THERE SHE BLOWS

In March 2002 the British journal *Lloyd's List*, which has provided shipping news since the 1730s, announced that from then on it would stop calling ships 'she' and refer to them as 'it'. It was the end of an era. Traditionally in Britain, ships have always been referred to as though they are female, even if they have a masculine-sounding name such as HMS *Endeavour*.

No one is entirely sure why this tradition sprang up. There are lots of theories, from the idea that a female ship was the perfect complement to her male crew to the notion that a sailing ship viewed in profile is a symphony of womanly curves. It is also thought that ships were originally dedicated to goddesses and placed in their care, so were referred to accordingly. Alternatively, perhaps it's because the curve of a ship's hull and the sense of protection that she creates has a feminine quality.

Whatever the reason, referring to a ship as 'it' may conform to political correctness but it lacks all trace of romance.

THE SHIP'S CAT

Everyone onboard ship has to pull their weight, from the captain down to the smallest member of the crew. Some crew members might have four legs rather than the regulation two, but that doesn't make them any the less valuable.

We have been taking cats onboard ship since at least the days of the Ancient Egyptians, thanks to their efficiency at catching vermin, such as rats and mice. Cats also provide companionship to sailors who are far away from home, and their agility helps them to get around a ship in even the roughest weather. Unfortunately, the Royal Navy banned cats and all other animals from their ships in 1975, citing worries over hygiene. But until then, the ship's cat was a regular feature. Some have even been so brave that they've been awarded medals for gallantry.

One of the most celebrated ship's cats was Simon, a black and white tom also known as Blackie to his fellow sailors, who became a very young member of the Royal Navy's HMS *Amethyst* in 1948 after she docked at Hong Kong for supplies. Simon was smuggled onboard by an ordinary seaman, but luckily the captain approved when he finally discovered Simon's presence and was happy for him to stay. Simon was assiduous in his duties, even to the point of leaving his prizes laid out for inspection on the captain's bunk. When he was ready for a nap, he saw nothing wrong in curling up in the captain's upturned cap.

In April 1949 the *Amethyst* was given orders to sail up the Yangtze River in order to relieve a sister ship which was guarding the British Embassy in Nanking from a Communist uprising. The *Amethyst* was shelled en route, which killed 25 crew members including the captain. Simon was badly injured by the blast and wasn't found for days. His wounds were tended by the ship's medical officer and he gradually recovered. He began to resume his regular duties, and sat respectfully on deck during the funeral service for his dead crew members. The *Amethyst* was being detained by the Communists and morale was low. The rat population had increased dramatically while Simon was on sick leave, seriously endangering the precious food supplies that were left. One particularly large and hungry rat, nicknamed Mao Tse- tung, was deemed too vicious for Simon to tackle in his convalescent state, but he finally came across the rat and despatched him. The crew were so delighted that they promoted Simon to Able Seacat Simon.

The *Amethyst* eventually managed to escape her Communist captors and made it to open waters. During a special celebration, Able Seacat Simon was awarded a campaign ribbon along with his fellow crew member, a dog called Peggy. More honours were to come. In August 1949 it was confirmed that Simon had become the first cat to be awarded the Dickin Medal, a medal for gallantry presented to members of the animal kingdom by the People's Dispensary for Sick Animals. Simon was still onboard ship, so had yet to receive the medal, but in the meantime he wore a collar in the colours of the medal ribbon.

Sadly, Simon never lived to receive his medal. After the *Amethyst* reached Plymouth that November, Simon was put in quarantine in Surrey for six months. He soon came down with a virus that his body, still weakened from its war wounds, couldn't fight. He died late the same month, only a few days before he was due to be presented with his medal. He appears on the Roll of Honour with the following citation: 'Served on the HMS *Amethyst* during the Yangtze incident, disposing of many rats though injured by shell blast. Throughout the incident his behaviour was of the highest order, although the blast was capable of making a hole over a foot in diameter in a steel plate.'

Simon died a hero, and his obituary even appeared in *Time* magazine. To date, he is the only cat to have received the prestigious Dickin Medal.

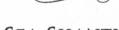

SEA SHANTIES

In the early days of the Second World War, a radio programme called *Music While You Work* kept the workers cheerful. It also increased production because everyone worked in time to the music.

Not that there is anything new in this idea. Back in the days when ships were powered by a combination of human muscle and sail, sailors were encouraged to sing while they worked. The shanties, as these work songs were called (from the French *chanter*, meaning 'to sing'), had a brisk, steady rhythm that helped to while away the time and fostered a sense of togetherness. Most importantly, they enabled the crew to haul on the lines (the nautical term for ropes) in a coordinated effort. Today shanties have fallen out of use as work songs and the Royal Navy has banned them in case the singing drowns out any commands that may be issued.

Most sea shanties involve one person (the shantyman) calling and the rest of the crew responding. They can be divided into several different categories, according to the nature of the work that was carried out while the shanties were being sung.

Short-haul, or sheet, shanties

These were the ideal accompaniment when giving quick but powerful pulls on a line for a short time, such as when shortening or unfurling sails.

Halyard, or long-haul, shanties

These were sung during heavy work involving some preparation time between each pull, such as when hoisting topsails. This sort of shanty usually has a chorus at the end of each line.

Capstan, or windlass, shanties

Capstan shanties were sung for lengthy or repetitive tasks, such as when raising or dropping the anchor. They got their name from the capstan, which is the giant winch that raises and drops a ship's anchor. These shanties have a smooth rhythm.

Forebitters, or fo'c's'le, shanties

Shanties are work songs, but forebitters are ballads sung by sailors when they were off-duty. Sailors often sang them while relaxing in the fo'c's'le ('forecastle'), which is where they slept, or on deck near the fore bitts, which were large wooden posts.

GUERNSEYS, GANSEYS AND ARANS

Stitches can tell stories. They certainly do in the case of traditional Guernsey jumpers. These have been worn by sailors since the 17th century and they are specially designed to be durable, waterproof and to allow plenty of movement. After all, if you're working hard on your fishing vessel you don't want to hear any telltale rips when you bend over too far and neither do you want to get a chill in your kidneys because your jumper rides up every time you raise your hands above your head. You need to wear something that is designed specifically for all the tasks you will be carrying out.

✖ Guernseys ✖

Guernseys have a long history. As their name suggests, they come from Guernsey in the Channel Islands. Originally, the Guernsey knitting industry produced stockings, and two of its most illustrious 16th-century customers were Elizabeth I and her estranged cousin Mary, Queen of Scots. The story goes that Mary wore a pair of Guernsey stockings at her execution (which was ordered by Elizabeth).

After stockings came jerseys (a name that originates from the neighbouring island of Jersey) that were tightly knitted from oiled wool. They were designed for the local fishermen, with each area of the island creating its own distinctive pattern of stitches. These patterns were not only decorative: they had the more practical (and grisly) function of identifying the origins of shipwrecked or drowned sailors. The jumpers were knitted in the round on four needles, to prevent seams splitting or chafing when they were damp, and they had diamond-shaped gussets under the arms for ease of movement.

Guernseys were knitted from unscoured wool, meaning that its natural lanolin content hadn't been removed. At this point, the wool was undyed. But that changed during the Napoleonic Wars when Admiral Lord Nelson was so impressed by the weatherproof qualities of these jumpers that he recommended they should become part of the uniform for sailors in the Royal Navy. The jumpers were supplied, but had to be dyed navy blue.

What were originally lots of different patterns for Guernseys eventually were distilled into the distinctive style we know today. Some of their features are said to represent different aspects of the sea. The ribbing at the top of the sleeves is reminiscent of a ship's rope ladder. The panels of garter stitch represent the waves breaking on the shore, and the raised seams across the shoulders are meant to look like ropes.

❧ Ganseys ❧

Guernseys aren't the only style of jumper associated with shipping. The gansey, whose name is a dialect variation of 'Guernsey', originated in the north of England and in Scotland. Although they are similar to Guernseys in shape they are much more extravagantly patterned with beautiful cables, diamonds and herringbones. The pattern isn't only for decoration – the extra layers of tightly knitted wool give added protection, particularly across the chest.

Just as with Guernseys, some of these patterns were references to various facets of the seafaring life, such as anchors, ropes and nets. Others were more personal. The 'marriage lines' pattern which originated in Filey, Yorkshire, consists of zigzags that indicate the ups and downs of so-called wedded bliss. Unlike Guernseys, which are traditionally made from oiled wool, ganseys are knitted with tightly worsted wool.

The main body of the gansey is knitted on four needles. The stitches around the armholes are used as the foundation row for the sleeves, which are often patterned to the elbow, with plain stocking stitch down to the cuffs. This makes it easy to unpick the frayed cuffs and re-knit them. The cuffs are traditionally very tightly knitted to prevent them getting caught in machinery (which could be fatal), and they stop short of the wrists to avoid them getting soaking wet. Even today, a hand-knitted gansey is a work of art.

❧ Arans ❧

Ireland is another part of the British Isles with a traditional style of hand-knitted sweaters. As with Guernseys, the Aran sweater took its name from its place of origin. In this case it is the Aran Islands off the west coast of Ireland. It is sometimes claimed that the sweater came from the Isle of Arran in Scotland, but this is wrong.

For centuries, fishermen from the Aran Islands wore their own style of traditional gansey with its beautiful patterns. These had special meanings, although there is some dispute about what exactly these were. Were they religious, did they represent facets of the fishermen's lives or were they designed to bring good luck at sea? The chunky, highly patterned jumper that is now known as an Aran sweater is a much more recent arrival, and is thought to have started life in the early 1900s. Even so, it has many lovely patterns, and its complex network of stitches guarantee to keep the wearer cosy and warm, even if they are far from the sea.

I Name This Ship...

The naming of a ship is a solemn business. You are committing her to the waves, where who knows what adventures will befall her, and you therefore want to invoke the blessings of any deities who happen to be listening.

Humans have been doing it for millennia. The Ancient Greeks relied on Poseidon, the god of the sea, to protect them when they were on his waters. When launching a ship they would honour the gods by drinking wine and pouring water on the deck. The Romans did the same, but directed their prayers to Neptune.

When Christianity arrived in Britain, ships were still blessed with wine and water but the procedure was conducted in accordance with the new religion. Some of these ceremonies could be elaborate and lengthy. But after the Reformation of the 16th century, when Protestantism became the national religion and elaborate Catholic ceremonies were against the law, these rituals disappeared. Gone was the holy water that was once sprinkled on the deck. Instead, as the ship was being launched a toast was drunk from a special vessel called a standing cup made from precious metals, the rest of the alcohol was thrown on to the deck and the standing cup was then tossed overboard, where it was a case of finder's keepers. Eventually, the standing cup was caught in a net each time it went over the side so it could be reused. It went out of use in the late 1600s and was replaced by a bottle of alcohol that was traditionally broken across the bow of the ship.

Doing this hasn't always been as easy as you might imagine. Although bottles have a nasty habit of breaking when you don't want them to, they can be surprisingly resilient when thrown against the side of a ship. The problem is that an unbroken bottle immediately bestows bad fortune on the ship – and, for superstitious sailors, any harbingers of doom should be avoided at all costs.

Today a ship is launched with a bottle of champagne broken across her bows. These bottles have to be very strong to withstand the air pressure created by the champagne, which means they're likely to bounce off a ship unless they're doctored first. One way to do this is to score the bottle with a glass cutter, as that creates a tiny fault that will help the bottle to smash to smithereens.

If you are ever in the happy position of choosing a bottle of champagne with which to name your own ship, go for quantity rather than quality. Buy the biggest bottle of fizz you can afford – a jeroboam will break more easily than a magnum – and give it a good shake before hurling it at your pride and joy. You most definitely want it to break. As it's often been said that owning and sailing a boat is like standing in a cold shower while ripping up £50 notes, you will need all the help from the gods that you can get.

A Ship's Figurehead

Sailors have been decorating the bows of their ships for thousands of years. The Ancient Egyptians did it, although we aren't certain of their reasons for it. Perhaps these were magical symbols, intended to bring good fortune to the sailors during their voyage, or maybe they had a spiritual significance. The designs often involved eyes, because it was important for the ship to see her way through the waves. And the practice continued down the centuries, because if anyone needs good fortune and the blessings of a god it is a crew of sailors putting out to sea.

In medieval times, figureheads flourished. Not only did they continue the practice of asking for divine help at sea, they also enabled illiterate sailors to recognise their own ship. Changes to ship designs in the 14th century made it difficult to fix a figurehead to the ship's bow so it was replaced by a design painted directly on to the hull. But the figurehead returned in the second half of the 15th century, thanks to another change in the design of ships.

Very grand, important naval vessels had equally grand figureheads. They were beautifully ornate, especially during the Baroque period of the 17th and 18th centuries when they were made first from elm and later from oak. Lions often featured heavily, especially on British ships, not only because of their high-ranking status in the animal kingdom and their fearsome ability as predators but also because a lion features on the royal coat of arms.

Fashions come and go in everything, including ships' figureheads. The Royal Navy began to frown on over-ornamented ships, with the lowest ranks of warships being the first to have their decoration scaled down so it was much more functional. Even so, the top ships of the fleet were allowed to retain their figureheads. The final three battle-ships in the British fleet to carry figureheads were HMS *Warrior* (launched in December 1860), HMS *Black Prince* (launched in February 1861) and HMS *Rodney* (launched in October 1884).

While lions roared in the Navy, merchant fleets often preferred to grace their ships with beautiful women. One of the most famous is the *Cutty Sark*, which was a tea clipper first launched in November 1869. Her figurehead is Nannie the Witch, a character taken from Robert Burns' poem 'Tam O'Shanter'. In the poem, Nannie is described as wearing a 'cutty sark', which was a short shirt. And that is how the ship got her name.

DOWN THE HATCH!

B ack in the days of sail, it was tough work being a sailor. You needed all the encouragement you could get and this often came out of a barrel.

For centuries, until 1970 when the practice was abolished, sailors in the Navy were given a daily tot of alcohol. This was originally brandy or beer, both of which were safer to drink than fresh water, which tended to turn putrid during long sea voyages. All this changed after Jamaica became an English colony in 1655, and by 1731 rum had replaced brandy on sea voyages. British sailors were given half a pint (0.29 litres) of rum a day, receiving half their allowance in the morning and half at night.

The sailors were delighted but the Admiralty less so. In 1740 Admiral Vernon ordered that a sailor's daily rum ration should be diluted with two pints (1.1 litres) of water in a probably vain attempt to reduce the drunkenness onboard his ship. Vernon was known to his men as 'Old Grogram', so the watered down rations were soon called 'grog'.

On special occasions, the men were given an extra tot of rum as a form of celebration. Very rarely, it was to reward them for hard work. This extra tot was announced as an order to 'splice the mainbrace'. The mainbrace is the rope or pulley attached to the lowest yard on the mainmast of a square-rigged ship, and it controls the mainsail which is biggest and heaviest of all the sails on the ship. It therefore involved a great deal of effort, which was very occasionally rewarded with a refreshing tot of something alcoholic.

Further measures to limit the drunkenness onboard ship (no wonder one popular maritime song is called 'What shall we do with a drunken sailor?') were introduced in 1850. The rum ration was reduced to one-eighth of a pint (71ml). It finally vanished altogether on 1 August 1970.

As well as calling their rum ration 'grog', sailors also called it 'Nelson's blood'. That's because they wrongly believed that after his death at the Battle of Trafalgar, Admiral Lord Nelson's body was preserved in a barrel of rum during the voyage back to England and that sailors guarding the cask had helped themselves to the odd tot. This was referred to as 'tapping the Admiral'. In fact, Nelson's body was placed in a leaguer, which was the biggest cask onboard the *Victory*, and filled with brandy. This brandy was replaced several times before the ship reached England because as the body rotted it released gases that threatened to burst the cask wide open. It's hard to believe that any sailor, no matter how thirsty – or patriotic – would have fancied a nip from that particular cask.

LEGENDS

Until he came to a mermaid
At the bottom of the deep blue sea
Singing Rule Britannia, Britannia rule the waves
Britons never, never, never shall be
married to a mermaid
At the bottom of the deep blue sea.

'OH! TWAS IN THE BROAD ATLANTIC', ANONYMOUS

WHERE GIANTS WALKED?

People come from all over the world to see the Giant's Causeway near Bushmills in County Antrim, Northern Ireland. They marvel at the tens of thousands of interlocking basalt columns that lead out to sea. The causeway is a breathtaking sight, and the real reason for its existence is just as astonishing as the local legends that account for its existence.

The facts are a fascinating reminder of how life in the British Isles is a lot more peaceful than it was millions of years ago. That's because the Giant's Causeway is the residue of the volcanic eruptions that took place between 50 and 60 million years ago in a huge basaltic lava plain known as the Thulean Plateau. Geophysicists believe that it broke up when the Atlantic Ocean was being formed, with sections of it ending up in Scotland and Northern Ireland, among other places. Some of the basalt columns are a majestic sight, standing about 36 feet (12 metres) high. Millennia of weathering from the sea, wind and rain have eroded some of the stacks into strange shapes and earned them names such as the Giant's Boot, the Chimney Stacks, the Harp and the Organ.

The mythology about the Giant's Causeway is just as intriguing, and the clue to the story lies in its name. According to local legend, the causeway was created by the mythical Irish warrior Fionn mac Cumhall (Finn McCool) when he wanted to get to Scotland so he could fight the Scottish warrior Benandonner. But Fionn fell asleep halfway there and when he didn't arrive in Scotland Benandonner came looking for him. There are variations on the story at this point, but the gist of it is that the Scotsman mistook the sleeping Fionn for his baby son and fled back home, believing that if the baby was that huge his father must be absolutely gigantic. Benandonner ran, ripping up the basalt columns as he went to stop Fionn following him.

Presumably Benandonner became braver the further he got from the sleeping Fionn, because it seems that by the time he reached the Scottish island of Staffa in the Inner Hebrides he felt confident enough to leave the basalt causeway where it was. And here it remains, at the entrance to what is now known as Fingal's Cave. This is a magnificent cathedral of basalt columns that was formed during the same volcanic eruptions that created the Giant's Causeway. It is named after the poem 'Fingal' by the 19th-century poet James MacPherson and it inspired 'The Hebrides Overture' (1830) by Felix Mendelssohn. The character of Fingal was based on that of Fionn mac Cumhall, so there are literary as well as geological links between the deserted beauty of Staffa and the astonishing hexagonal steps of the Giant's Causeway.

THE MYSTERIES OF ST MICHAEL'S MOUNT

Cornwall is a county rich in legends, and the gloriously rugged coastline, huge bays and fascinating geology all contribute to the sense of being in an ancient and rather mysterious land.

One place that is suitably atmospheric is St Michael's Mount in south-western Cornwall. The setting of a castle on an island out in Mount's Bay is magical enough, but when you add the materialisation of the Archangel Michael, the exploits of Jack the Giant Killer and a submerged forest, you have the recipe for a place of great mystery.

The island gets its name from the Archangel St Michael, who is said to have appeared to a group of fishermen at the end of the 5th century. However, churches built on hills are traditionally dedicated to either St Michael or St Catherine, so it may be that the legend owes more to religious custom.

Not surprisingly, a religious community developed here, and in the 11th century the land was given to the Benedictine monastery of Mont-St-Michel in Normandy. It looks very similar to St Michael's Mount, the names are the same, and they are only separated by a relatively short stretch of the English Channel. The Cornish island returned to English hands in the 14th century but the monastery was closed in 1425. It became a castle but was still a place of pilgrimage. In 1588 it was where the first beacon was lit to signal the arrival of the Spanish Armada. Today it is owned by the National Trust and is open to the public.

According to legend, Mount's Bay was once dry land covered in thick forest. A giant called Cormoran wanted to build a stronghold here so he instructed his wife, Cormelian, to collect boulders of white granite. He went to sleep while his wife put the boulders in her apron. But Cormelian found this such hard work that she decided to pick up greenstone boulders instead. When Cormoran woke up he was so angry that he kicked his wife's apron. The strings broke and the greenstone she was carrying flew out. You can still see it at the start of the man-made causeway that leads to St Michael's Mount, which was said to be Cormoran's fortress. He would creep out at night and steal the local farmers' sheep and cows so he could eat them.

However, Cormoran didn't live in his fortress for long. One night, Jack the Giant Killer stole on to the Mount and dug a deep pit which he covered with straw. Then he blew his horn to entice Cormoran out of his home. The giant rushed out and tumbled into the pit, at which point Jack cut off his head with a single blow from his axe. The locals amply rewarded him with a gold-embroidered belt and a beautiful sword.

OF MERMAIDS AND MERMEN

Whatever you might think about the existence or otherwise of mermaids and mermen, stories about them are astonishingly similar no matter which part of the world they come from.

These creatures are generally thought to have human bodies and fishes' tails. According to legend, a mermaid or merman has no soul and can only gain one by marrying a mortal. This task is fairly easy for mermaids who are traditionally extremely beautiful, with long lustrous hair that they comb enticingly, and wonderful singing voices with which they lure sailors to their underwater homes. Mermen are usually considered to be less alluring – maybe they're the rough trade of the folklore world – but they have their collective eye on lovely women who can give them the souls they crave.

Regardless of whether you encounter a mermaid or a merman, you must treat him or her with kindness and consideration to avoid being cursed. You must also hope that the sea creature doesn't make any amorous advances towards you, as it's extremely bad luck to spurn their romantic overtures. Yet the other option means that you will have to bid farewell to your earthly life for ever more. So it's best to avoid them altogether.

❧ The Merfolk family ❧

Tales of mermaids abound around the British coastline but are particularly prevalent in Cornwall and Scotland. For a long time it was even claimed that one Scottish family called Clan McVeagh, from Sutherland in Scotland, was descended from a union between a mermaid and a mortal.

❧ The Murkle mermaid ❧

Mermaids have often been accused of tricking humans, but in Murkle in Highland, at the tip of the north-eastern Scottish mainland, some dual trickery was involved. A mermaid fell in love with a local fisherman and gave him wonderful gifts of gold and jewellery. But when she discovered that her perfidious lover was passing on these gifts to human girls, she took action. The story goes that she took him to Dwarwick Head in Dunnet Bay and led him down to a cave that was crammed with treasure taken from all the ships that had ever been wrecked in the Pentland Firth. While he was gazing at all these riches she began to sing to him, and it was such a sweet song that he soon fell asleep. When he woke, he discovered to his horror that he had been chained to the floor of the cave with golden fetters, and it's said that he's still being kept there by his jealous mermaid lover.

❧ The Mermaid of Zennor ❧

The last place that you might expect to find a mermaid is in a church, but that's where you'll see the so-called Mermaid of Zennor. There is a carving of her on the end of a bench in St Senara church in the small village of Zennor in Cornwall, and a mermaid is also depicted on a bronze dial, dated 1737, on the south side of the church. Legend has it that several centuries ago a beautiful young woman would occasionally attend services at the church. Whenever she was there all the male choristers did their best to sing as melodiously as possible, but the best singer by far was a handsome young man called Matthew Trewella. One Sunday morning after church the beautiful woman invited Matthew to go for a walk with her. He did, but he never returned. Many years later, it is said that a ship dropped anchor in nearby Pendower Cove. The captain was astonished to see a beautiful mermaid emerge from the waves and ask him politely to shift his anchor as it was blocking the way to the undersea house she shared with her husband, Matthew, and their children.

❧ The curse of the Merfolk ❧

Not all mermaids have been so easy-going. In the 5th century, a severe fish famine in Conway in Wales was blamed on a mermaid who had been washed ashore during a violent storm. Even though she begged them to return her to the sea, the fishermen who found her refused to do it. She cursed the people of Conway with her dying breath, saying they would always be poor.

It was a merman who is said to have once caused problems for the fishermen sailing around Portgordon in north-east Scotland. He apparently had extraordinarily long arms, and he was considered to be a very bad omen so any sailor who caught sight of him would head back to port immediately. Perhaps the sailors were worried that he would entice their women down to his underwater domain while they were away at sea.

THE CREATURES OF ORKNEY

According to legend, the sea contains many strange creatures that are part animal, part human. Merfolk – mermaids and mermen who can only regain their lost souls by marrying mortals – are the best known but they aren't the only mythical sea beings by any means. The islanders of Orkney know of at least two other creatures – selkiefolk and finfolk.

The stories change slightly with successive generations but originally both selkiefolk and finfolk were considered to be malicious creatures that should be avoided at all costs. Since then, selkiefolk have been painted in a much more flattering and benevolent light, while finfolk have retained their original reputation for being harmful and justifiably feared.

➤ Selkiefolk ➤

Selkiefolk were said by some to be the souls of people who had drowned and were allowed to return to human form once a year.

Another theory was that they were a type of fallen angel, doomed to live as animals until the Day of Judgement released them. A third belief was that they were humans who had blotted their copybooks to such a serious degree that they were doomed to live as grey seals ('seal' is *selkie* in Orcadian dialect) and could only revert to their original form every now and then.

There is some dispute about how often they were able to do this – some people believed that selkies could shape-shift from seal to human every nine days while others thought it was an annual event performed on Midsummer's Eve. Selkies often celebrated this accomplishment by dancing, naked and alone, on moonlit beaches. Regardless of when this shape-shifting happened, it was essential that the selkie kept a firm grip on their discarded seal skin, otherwise they wouldn't be able to return to their original form and escape to their natural home in the sea.

As might be expected from creatures that are really seals, both selkie men and women were very attractive to humans. So much so that it wasn't unknown for a woman to deliberately entice a selkie-man by going down to the shore at high tide and shedding seven tears into the sea. The selkie man would emerge from the sea, remove his sealskin and then take off the woman's clothes for what a 19th-century folklorist described as 'unlawful love'. Any children that arrived as a result of this 'unlawful' union were believed to have webbed hands and feet, and the webs would grow back no matter how often they were cut away.

As selkies had such a reputation for sexual adventure, it is easy to see how an unwanted pregnancy might be conveniently blamed on enchantment by a male selkie.

❧ Finfolk ❧

Stories of selkiefolk aren't only confined to the Orkney Islands, as they are also told in the Western Isles, northern and western Scotland, and Ireland. But finfolk are creatures that apparently lived at the bottom of the sea near Orkney in their ancestral and truly fantastic home of Finfolkaheem. This was a magical and special place, with massive crystal halls and floors littered with giant pearls. They retreated here each winter to avoid the bitter weather, and would emerge in the summer to live on their special island of Hildaland – a magical realm that was said to appear and then disappear when necessary.

Like selkiefolk, the finfolk were skilled shape-shifters. They were also malevolent sorcerers who were rightly feared by Orcadians. If they took a fancy to a human, they would spirit away him or her, taking their captive off to live with them for ever more. Presumably, sailors who were lost at sea or people who were swept away by the waves in storms were said to have been taken by the finfolk.

The finfolk themselves disappeared soon after Christianity arrived in Scotland, as it was said that they couldn't survive in a land where the true Gospel was preached. Their magical island of Hildaland disappeared with them but has remained a fascinating topic of Orcadian folklore ever since.

LOST LANDS

As their name suggests, the British Isles consists of many islands. Hundreds of them, in fact. But if legend is correct, there were once more of them and some of them had magical powers.

The Orkney Islands consists of over 70 islands, ranging from Mainland, which is the largest, to tiny islets that are only inhabited by birds. But tradition tells us that many centuries ago there were at least two very special islands as well. They were special because they were able to appear and then disappear almost at will, so they were associated with magical powers.

⇒ Hildaland ⇐

One of these islands was Hildaland, which was said to be the summer residence of the feared finfolk – those sinister creatures that roamed the sea and were thought to steal humans. Some people believe that

Hildaland is really the tiny island of Eynhallow, which lies between the northern coast of Mainland and the southern coast of the much smaller Rousay.

Eynhallow is now uninhabited but in previous centuries it was considered to be a holy island. People lived on it until disease wiped out their settlement in the 1850s, and it still has the ruins of a 12th-century church. According to local legend, humans were only able to settle on the island after the terrible finfolk were evicted. The story goes that they were tricked into leaving by a farmer from Evie on Mainland, who was furious when the finfolk stole his wife. As soon as the finfolk and their cattle had left the island, the farmer carved nine crosses into the turf and encircled Eynhallow with nine rings of salt – two time-honoured ways of keeping evil at bay.

❧ Hether Blether ❧

This is the other magical Orkney island. Like Hildaland, it is associated with the finfolk but, unlike that island, it is said that the finfolk still live on Hether Blether. It lies further out to sea than Eynhallow, and is still magically able to appear and disappear. The only way for its magical powers to be broken would be if a mortal man were able to set foot on it, but that would be a dangerous business. In order to avert bewitchment and capture, he must hold a piece of steel (a protection against witchcraft) in his hand while sailing towards the island, and must never once take his eyes off it. Presumably, as Hether Blether is still hidden, no human has yet been able to manage this feat.

❧ Lyonesse ❧

Today the tip of Land's End in Cornwall gives vast and captivating views of the sea that surrounds this stretch of coastline. But according to legend, the ocean hides a secret – the lost land of Lyonesse. Apparently, the Isles of Scilly are all that remain of what was once a huge island, complete with villages and churches, that was drowned by the sea approximately 1,000 years ago. Some fishermen have even claimed to have dredged up pieces of old Lyonesse buildings in their nets, and if you can hear bells ringing on stormy nights it is said that you might be hearing the submerged bells of Lyonesse churches. Legend has it that only one man, named Trevilian, survived when Lyonesse was flooded by the tide. He escaped on a white horse.

❧ Cantre'r Gwaelod ❧

Wales, a country steeped in Celtic myth, lays claim to at least two lost lands. Cardigan Bay is a massive, curved bay on the west coast of Wales and is said to cover an equally enormous stretch of land that once lay between Ramsay Island and Bardsey Island. Stories differ about what this land was. Some stories claim that it is the lost land of Maes Gwyddno, which was submerged in the 5th century by an over-flowing well.

Other tales say that it was called Cantre'r Gwaelod, or the Lowland Hundred, and was claimed by the tide when its sea defences failed, thanks to the ineptitude of a man called Seithenyn who was supposed to shut the sluices each night but failed to do so because he was drunk. What is so fascinating about this story is that low tide between Borth and Ynyslas in Cardigan Bay sometimes reveals the petrified stumps of a wide variety of trees. Radiocarbon dating of these trees suggests that the trees near Borth died about 3500 BC, while those near Ynyslas are relatively newer, having died in about 1500 BC.

❧ Tyno Helig ❧

Conway Bay on the north-west coast of Wales also has its secrets. Legend says that the sea hides the land of Tyno Helig, which was submerged in the 7th century. A small cluster of rocks visible from Penmaenmawr is said to be all that's left of the palace of Prince Helig ap Glannawg, who owned this once fertile land. His palace was called Llys Helig. Apparently, his kingdom was claimed by the sea as divine retribution after his black-hearted and greedy daughter, Gwendud, was involved in the murder of a rich nobleman. It is said that very low tides reveal the ruins of the old palace.

Regardless of whether this is true, the legend of the lost palace has lived on in a local place name, because an area on the western slopes of Great Ormes Head is still called Llys Helig.

SUPERSTITIONS

Full fathom five thy father lies;
Of his bones are coral made:
Those are pearls that were his eyes:
Nothing of him that doth fade,
But doth suffer a sea-change
Into something rich and strange

THE TEMPEST, WILLIAM SHAKESPEARE

SETTING SAIL

A wise sailor heeded various superstitions when beginning a sea voyage, and some of us still do. One of the most enduring superstitions is to avoid setting sail on a Friday, because of its connection with Christ's crucifixion. Setting sail on Friday the 13th is even worse and not to be contemplated by any sane person. Something else to be avoided is to begin a sea voyage on New Year's Eve, as that is traditionally the day on which Judas Iscariot hanged himself.

Choosing the right day for the voyage is a wise precaution but the superstitions don't end there. You should never step on to a ship with your left foot because that will court disaster. And on the subject of feet, you should avoid flat-footed people when beginning a voyage. If the worst comes to the worst, you can avert trouble by speaking to them first. The same rule of speaking first applies if you encounter someone with red hair, especially if they happen to have flat feet as well. When you are safely onboard ship, don't throw a stone overboard while the ship is putting out to sea because that would ensure she never returns to port. You mustn't look over your shoulder at the port you're leaving behind, either, because that will bring bad luck.

Something else to avoid is carrying a bunch of flowers as you board the ship. There is always the danger that they could later be used as a funeral wreath because of a death at sea. You should keep away from any priests who are onboard, too, as they wear traditionally wear black and officiate at funerals. The last thing you want to do is to tempt fate by talking to them.

When you're safely out of the harbour, you must be careful about which birds you look at. It's lucky to see curlews and swallows, but you're in deep trouble if you spot any cormorants. It's even worse if you see a shark following the ship because that is said to be a sure sign of a forthcoming death.

There are many things to do onboard ship, but two that you should try to avoid are cutting your nails or hair. The trimmings were once offered to the Roman goddess Prosperina, but you are now sailing through Neptune's kingdom and the last thing you want is to make him jealous. He is, after all, the god of the sea.

THE DREADED ALBATROSS

According to maritime superstition, the albatross brings both good and bad luck. It can bestow good weather but it can also bring storms. It also carries something very precious – the souls of drowned sailors – so this huge bird must be treated with respect.

In his poem *The Rime of the Ancient Mariner*, Samuel Taylor Coleridge described the impact that an albatross had on one ship in particular. The ship was sailing towards the South Pole when it encountered an icy and foggy world of strange shapes and terrifying noises. Then an albatross appeared and the sailors fed it. The ice split, the helmsman steered the ship through the ice sheets and 'a good south wind' sprang up that carried the crew to safety. But the Ancient Mariner, the teller of the tale, shot the albatross and, in doing so, brought a terrible curse upon the ship and all the men. The crew hung the dead albatross around the Ancient Mariner's neck as a punishment, but worse was to come, including the arrival of a skeleton ship.

This belief in the albatross as a bird of ill omen has persisted. In July 1959 a ship called the *Calpean Star* docked in Liverpool with engine trouble. The crew were far from happy because the ship was carrying an albatross bound for a zoo, and they blamed its presence for the run of bad luck that had dogged them all the way from the Antarctic. The ship was abandoned off Montevideo the following year after an explosion in her boiler room.

WHISTLING UP A STORM

No matter how jaunty you might be feeling while onboard ship, the last thing you should do is to whistle a happy tune. Sailors don't like it because it runs the risk of whistling up some bad weather. If you're lucky, you'll just get away with a gusty wind. If you're really unlucky, you'll invite a gale or tempest. The only time when it's a good idea to whistle is if your sailing ship is becalmed and you need the wind to getting her moving again.

There is a good historical reason for this nautical superstition about whistling onboard ship. The sound of someone whistling might easily have been confused with the sound of the bosun piping a command on his whistle – something that could have very serious consequences.

A dislike of whistling isn't only experienced onboard ship. It is also a superstition backstage in theatres. That's because many stage-hands used to be sailors who were hired while their ship was in port. After all, men who were accustomed to climbing the rigging of sailing ships would be perfectly at home clambering about in the theatrical rigging backstage. And just as onboard ship, theatrical commands were given with a series of whistles. So a stagehand whistling while he went about his work might confuse the rest of the stage crew or the actors. And the superstition persists. Today, even though instructions are given to theatre crews using a system of lights, it's still considered unlucky to whistle in a theatre.

GHOST SHIPS

Imagine the scene. A misty night, with the moon a muted smudge behind thick clouds. The wind blowing, making the sails of your ship snap and flap. The distant voices of your fellow sailors, reassuring on this lonely night. The creaking of the ship's hull as she rides the waves. You know other ships are out there on the sea but you can't see them. It's too dark. And then a ship hoves into view.

But something about her isn't right. As you strain your eyes in the vain hope of seeing more clearly, you realise with a start that the ship is emitting a strange green light. You've never seen anything like it before. You're about to shout, 'Ship ahoy!' when, to your astonishment, she vanishes. You lean over the side of the ship, so far over that you're in danger of tumbling down into the sea. The moon, which has been hidden by clouds, suddenly breaks free and shines her light on the waves. But what's happened to the ship? She was there a minute ago and now she's gone.

And then you ask yourself a question you hardly dare put into words. Have you just seen a ghost ship? And if so, are you doomed?

Maritime folklore is full of unsettling stories of things you don't want to encounter, ranging from sirens whose beautiful singing lures sailors to their death to terrifying kraken that rise out of the sea and devour entire ships with one gulp of their hideous mouths. Ghost ships are equally unnerving, because they are said to sail the seas for ever, never able to make landfall. Their ghostly crew will deliver messages from you to the dead. Even worse, they are considered to be terrible portents of doom.

The Flying Dutchman is the most famous ghost ship of them all, inspiring stories by such writers as Sir Walter Scott and even an opera of the same name by Richard Wagner. Traditionally, her appearance always presages disaster, such as a terrifying storm or the death of a crewman.

Some stretches of sea are particularly notorious for sightings of ghost ships. One of these is a few miles off the coast from Deal in Kent. This is the massive and highly dangerous sandbank known as the Goodwin Sands. It lies close to very busy shipping lanes, and has been responsible for more than 2,000 wrecks. At least two ghost ships have been seen in these waters.

According to legend, the *Lady Lovibond* reappears every 50 years. She sank with all hands on 13 February 1748, when the first mate murdered the helmsman and steered the ship on to the sands. The captain had married the only woman that the first mate loved, and had added insult to injury by bringing his bride onboard for a honeymoon cruise to Oporto. This had already worried the sailors, who firmly believed that it was bad luck to have a woman onboard. Fifty years later, to the day, the captain of a coaster called *Edenbridge* wrote in the ship's log that she had almost collided with a three-masted schooner that was making straight for the Goodwin Sands. A fishing boat also saw her. In 1848 the appearance of the ghost ship was so convincingly lifelike that the Deal lifeboat was launched in an attempt to save her. It found nothing.

The other ghost ship reported to have been seen off the coast from Deal was the SS *Violet*, a cross-channel paddle steamer that ran on to the sands during a snowstorm in the late 19th century. In 1939 the man working as a lookout on the East Goodwin lightship summoned the Ramsgate lifeboat when he saw a paddle steamer run aground on the sands. When the lifeboat arrived, there was, of course, no sign of the steamer.

DOWN IN DAVY JONES' LOCKER

The sea is a vast and mysterious place. It's full of beauty but it has many dangers, too. And perhaps the most dangerous of them all is Davy Jones' locker. This is the sailor's name for the sea floor, which is where wrecked ships, lost treasure and human bones picked clean by fish eventually settle. In other words, Davy Jones' locker means death.

Maritime tradition has it that Davy Jones is the spirit of the sea, and an unfriendly one at that. Davy Jones is greedy for the souls of men and will do what he can to collect them. No wonder many sailors still avoid mentioning his name.

How did we arrive at this phrase? There are several theories, including the idea that 'Jones' is a corruption of 'Jonah', the prophet who jumped on a ship to escape God's command, was thrown overboard during a massive storm, was swallowed by a whale and eventually vomited out on to the shore. As for 'Davy', it might be a corruption of 'duffy', which is the West Indian word for a ghost.

There is one way of finding out how Davy Jones got his name, but it is drastic. And that's to ask him yourself, if you ever have the misfortune to meet him.

ACKNOWLEDGEMENTS

I've longed to write this book for a long time. I grew up by the sea in south-east England, where I loved messing about on the beach and going for boat trips round the lighthouse. Later on, I lived in a house built on the site of Admiral Lord Nelson's back garden in Merton, where I always hoped that the broken shards of china I found in the soil were remnants of the cups his fiery mistress, Emma Hamilton, used to throw at him in a rage. They probably weren't, but it was nice to dream. So it is a pleasure to finally get the chance to celebrate the sea in this book.

Many thanks to everyone at Ebury Press who gave me the opportunity to write it, and who have worked so hard on it, especially my editor, Charlotte Cole, my meticulous copy-editor Justine Taylor and Caitlin Doyle for her proofreading. I'd also like to thank my friend, Susan Chadwick, for giving me the benefit of her tremendous botanical expertise and then triple-checking I'd got my facts right. Any mistakes are mine, not hers. Thanks to my father-in-law, Basil Martin, who gave me two books on the Navy and the sea. And, as ever, I would also like to thank my stalwart agent, Chelsey Fox, and my husband, Bill Martin, who has once again put up with me being at my desk from dawn to dusk.

INDEX

Aldington Gang 186–7
Alexander II, Pope 160
Alfred the Great 191
Alice Through the Looking Glass (Carroll) 85
American War of Independence 194
Amethyst, HMS 244–5
Ancient Mariner 274–5
Anglo-Saxon Chronicle 157
Annales Rerum Angliae et Hiberniae Regnante Elizabetha (Camden) 164
Anne of Denmark 196
Anne Royal (ship) 196
Antonine Wall, 155
Ark Raleigh (ship) 196
Ark Royal, HMS 196–7
Arnold, Samuel J 215
Arthur, King 143
Arthur, William 184
Association, HMS 147
Atlantic Ocean 92, 135, 144–5, 163, 233, 234, 235, 259
August Bank Holiday Monday 17, 18

Bacon, Francis 133
bandstands 22–3
Bank Holidays Act (1871) 16–17

Bara Lafwr 78–9
Barbarossa, Hayreddin 161
Barbary corsairs/pirates 160–2
Barham, Rev. Richard H. 169
barnacles 99–100
Barry Island 184
bathing machines 24–6, 27
Battle Abbey 160
battleship rating system 197–8
Bayeux Tapestry 159
BBC 226
beach flags 38–9
beach games 55, 57–64
beach huts 27–8
beach volleyball 60–1
beachcombing 100–1
beachside reading 116–19
Beagle, HMS 167, 227
Beaufort, Francis 227
Beddoes, Thomas Lovell 281
Benandonner 259
'Best Beach Donkey' competition 57
Bibliothèque Nationale de France 173
Bikini Atoll 26
Bishops Cannings 186

Bitches 123
Black Prince, HMS 253
Blackbeard 173–5
Blackpool attractions 16, 21, 67
Blanchard, Jean-Pierre 136
Blue Water Round the World Rally 146
Board of Longitude 147–8
Board of Trade 227
bodyboarding 43
Bognor Regis 28
Bonaparte, Napoleon 164
boogie boarding 43
Botonologia: The British Physician (Turner) 80
Bounty, HMS 148
Bournemouth 17–18, 28
Boxing Day 17
boys' institutes 19
Brighthelmstone 15–16
Brighton Chair Pier 21
Brighton Farmhouse 16, 18, 117
Brighton Palace Pier 21
Brighton West Pier 21
Britannia 155
British Empire 149
British Isles, lost lands of 266–9

British Merchant Service 149
British waters, by name 137–40
Brookland, Battle of 186–7
bucket and spade 62–3, 64
Bulldog, HMS 167
Burns, Robert 253
Butlin, Billy 19–20
butterflies, types 94–5

Cailleach Bheur 124
Caister Holiday Camp 19
Calpean Star (ship) 275
Calvi, Battle of 199
Camden, William 164
Canute, King 157
Cape St Vincent, Battle of 194–5, 199
Carroll, Lewis 85
Carters of Prussia Cove 184–5
cats 23, 136, 217, 244–6
censorship committees 24
Channel Islands 165–7, 248
Channel Swimming Association (CSA) 136
Channel Swimming and Piloting Federation 136
Charlemagne 156
Charles II 30, 162, 192, 208, 226
Chesil Beach 131
Chichester, Sir Francis 145–6
Chimney Stacks (stack) 259

'chippies' 70–1
Christmas 17, 41
Church of England 144, 164
Churchill, Sir Winston 153
Cinque Ports 119–20, 191
Cinque Ports (ship) 150–1
clams 81
coastal birds 111–14
coastal hazards 122–30
coastal place names 140–2
coastal walks 114–16
coastguards 38
cockles 79, 81
Coleridge, Samuel Taylor 274
'Collier's Dying Child, The' (Farmer) 241
confectionary 67–8
contraband 169, 176, 177, 181–2, 183
Cook, Capt. James 148, 212, 213
Copenhagen, Battle of 199–200
Cormelian 261
Cormoran 261
Cornish heavy cake 73–4
Corryvreckan 124
crabs 40, 83, 96–8
CSA (Ltd) 136
Cumberland and Strathearn, Duke of 15
Cunningham Camp 19
Cunningham, Elizabeth 19
Cunningham, Joseph 19
customs duties 160, 176–7, 180, 184, 186

cuttlefish 100
Cutty Sark 146, 253

Darwin, Charles 227
Davy Jones' locker 11, 278–9
Dawes, Mr 162
Day of Judgement 265
deckchairs 27
Defoe, Daniel 150–1, 173
Dickens, Charles 71, 148
Dickin Medal 245, 246
'dippers' 25
Distinguished Service Cross 150
dogs 29, 245
Domesday Book 120
Donkey Sanctuary 58
Dover Traffic Separation System 135
Drake, Sir Francis 143, 146, 163, 192
'Drake's Drum' (Newbolt) 189
drinking toasts 201–2
ducks and drakes 58
Duke (ship) 151
Durdle Door 131

East Goodwin lightship 278
Easter 17
Economist 71
Edenbridge (ship) 277
Edward the Confessor 119, 157–9, 191
Edward I 122, 176
Edward III 191
Edward VIII 149
Effingham, Lord Howard of 192

Elizabeth I 70, 143, 208, 163–4, 192, 196, 208, 248
Elizabeth II 146
Endeavour, HMS 243
English Channel 108, 120, 135–6, 137, 159, 163, 164, 260
English Civil War 208
Experienced English Housekeeper, The (Raffald) 78

fairgrounds 67
Farmer, Edward 241
Farther Adventures of Robinson Crusoe, The (Defoe) 150
Ferdinand IV 199
ferries 135
figureheads, on ships 252–3
Fileux, Albert 136
finfolk 264, 265–6, 267
'Fingal' (MacPherson) 260
First World War 19, 149, 150, 202, 203
fish and chips 70–1
fish, types of 45–53
fishermen 11, 15, 27, 39–40, 73–4, 79, 83, 205, 210, 248, 250, 260, 262, 263, 268
fishing nets 39–40, 74
FitzRoy, Capt. (later Vice Admiral) Robert 226–7
flapjacks 76–7
Fleet Air Arm 192
Flying Dutchman (ghost ship) 277
Foley, Capt. Thomas 200

foods 68–83
Forkbeard, Sweyn 157
French cricket 59
fyke nets 39–40

Gardner, Rear Admiral Alan 213
General History of the Pyrates, A (Johnson) 173
George III 16, 148, 200
George IV 16
George V 28, 149
ghost ships 276–8
Giant's Boot (stack) 259
Giant's Causeway 259–60
gill nets 40
Gipsy Moth III (yacht) 145
Gipsy Moth IV (yacht) 145–6
Glannawg, Prince Helig ap 268
Glover-Kind, John H 22
Godwin, Earl 123, 158–9
Godwin, Harold 159
Godwin, Tostig 159
Golden Hind/Golden Hinde (ship) 143, 145
Goodwin Sands 123, 158, 277
Grace Dieu (ship) 191
Grahame, Kenneth 55
Gravelines, Battle of 163
Great Christopher (ship) 195
Great Fire of London 208
Great Northern Railway 13
Greenwich 146–8, 166

Greyfriars Monastery 121
Guinness Book of Records 58
gulls' eggs 80
Gwendud 268–9
Gwennap Head 124

Hadrian's Wall 155
Hamilton, Emma 199, 200, 201, 280
Hamilton, Sir William 199
Harald III 159
hard tack 210–11
Hardecnut, King 157
Hardy, Capt. Thomas 200
Hårfagre, Harald 157
Harold I 157
Harp (stack) 259
Harrison, John 146–8
Harrison, William 148
Hawkhurst Gang 183–4
'Hebrides Overture' (Mendelssohn) 260
Henry Grace à Dieu (ship) 191, 194
Henry V 191
Henry VII 191
Henry VIII 191, 193–4, 201
Henry, Prince 15
herbe de St-Pierre 79
Hitler, Adolf 166
holiday camps 18–20
Hollywood 171
Hornigold, Benjamin 174
Howard, Charles 196
Hudson River 144

'I Do Like to be Beside the Seaside' 22

Ice Age 108
ice cream 61, 75–6
imaginary places 116
impressment 208–10
Indomitable, HMS 197
Ingoldsby Legends, The
    (Ingoldsby) 169
Ingoldsby, Thomas 169
Insulae Britannicae 155
International Maritime
    Organization 135
Irresistible, HMS 196

Jack the Giant Killer
    260, 261
James I/VI 163, 196
James II 151
Jeeves and Wooster
    stories (Wodehouse)
    82
Jeffries, John 136
jellyfish 102–4
Jesus (ship) 191
jet-skiing 43
John, King 191
Johnson, Charles 173
Jolly Roger 172–3
Jonah 278
Jones, Capt.
    Christopher 144
Juan Fernandez Islands
    150
'Jumblies, The' (Lear)
    31
jumpers, types of 247–
    50

Kendall, Larcum 148
Kenfig 121–2
Keppel, Admiral 194
King Lear (Shakespeare)
    80
Kipling, Rudyard 178–9
kitesurfing 43

knickerbocker glory 75–
    6
Knight, Thomas 184
knots, types of 237–8

Lady Lovibond (ship)
    277
Land's End 124, 144,
    161, 267
laverbread 78–9
Lear, Edward 31
Lees, John 71
Leigh, HMS 21
Leith Chain Pier 21
lemonade, real 77–8
'Life on the Ocean
    Wave, A' (Arnold)
    215
lifeboats 38, 277, 278
lighthouses 12, 116,
    124, 125–30, 181,
    280
limpets 99
Lind, James 212
Little Dorrit (Dickens)
    148
Lloyd's List 243
Llys Helig palace 268–9
lobsters 40, 72–3, 83
Loch Ness Monster 131
longitude 146–8
Longitude Act (1773)
    148
Louis XVI 199
Lubbock, Sir John 16
lugworm casts 100–1
Lytham St Anne's 22

mac Cumhall, Fionn
    ('Finn McCool')
    259–60
McGill, Donald 23–4
MacPherson, James 260
McVeagh, Clan 262

Mademoiselle Fifi (cat)
    136
Magellan, Ferdinand
    143
Malin, Joseph 71
Manche, la, *see* English
    Channel
Mandubracius, King
    155
Mao Tsetung (rat) 245
Maritime and
    Coastguard Agency
    149
marshland 79–80, 91–2
Martello towers 164–5
Mary I 163, 193
Mary, Queen 28
Mary, Queen of Scots
    163, 248
Mary Rose 193–4
Maskelyne, Nevil 147–
    8
Mayflower (ship) 144–5
Memorial of Access
    (Bacon) 133
Mendelssohn, Felix 260
menus/recipes 69–70,
    74–8
Merchant
    Marine/Merchant
    Navy 149–50, 192,
    203
merfolk 261–4
Met Office 226–7
Middle Ages 207
Midsummer's Eve 265
Ministry of Food 71
modesty 25, 27, 41–2
Mods and Rockers 18
Moisant, John Bevins
    136
'Molly Malone' 65
Monmouth, Duke of
    151

Mont-St-Michel
    monastery 260
moonrakers 185, 186
Mootham, Capt. 162
Morning Herald 16
Mortemen 181
Murkle mermaid 262–3
Music While You Work
    246
mussels 81, 98

Nannie the Witch 253
Napoleonic Wars 16,
    194, 195, 197, 210,
    248
National Maritime
    Museum 148
National Piers Society
    21
National Service 210
nautical punishments,
    types of 238–40
nautical sayings 217–19
nautical terms 222–6,
    246
nautical time 220–1
Naval Discipline Act
    (1957) 204
navigational aids 146–8
navigational hazards
    125–30
Navy Board 192
Navy rum 253–5
Nelson, Admiral Lord
    Horatio (Viscount)
    194, 195, 198–201,
    248, 254, 280
Nelson, Frances
    ('Fanny') (née
    Nisbet) 199
Nelson, Horatia 199,
    201
Neptune (god) 250, 274
New Year 41, 221, 273

Newbolt, Sir Henry
    John 189
Newgate Prison 187
Nile, Baron Nelson of
    the 199
Nile, Battle of the 199
Nisbet, Frances
    ('Fanny') 199
Norman Conquest 11,
    158–60
North Carolina
    Maritime Museum
    175
North Sea 120, 135,
    137, 163, 196
Northern Lighthouse
    Board 125
Novomagius 155

Obscene Publications
    Act (1857) 24
Old Man of Hoy 131–2
Oliver Twist (Dickens) 71
Operation Green Arrow
    166
Organ (stack) 259
Ottoman Empire 161–2
Oulton, W C 25
owlers 185, 186
oysters 81–2

Pacific Ocean 82, 212
parasailing 43
Parker, Martin 109
Pegasus, HMS 196
Peggy (dog) 245
Pelican (ship) 143
People's Dispensary for
    Sick Animals
    (PDSA) 245
Pepys, Samuel 30, 161–
    2, 192, 197, 209
Philip II 162–3
Pickle, HMS 200

picnic menus 69–70
'pieces of eight' 175–6
Pietro Gimonde, Signor
    Pietro ('Signor
    Bologna') 30
Pilgrim Fathers 144–5
pirates 11, 160–2, 169,
    171–87
Pitman, Henry 151
political correctness 25,
    29, 243
Portuguese man-of-war
    103–4
Poseidon (god) 250
postcards 23–4
potted shrimps 74–5
press gang 208–10
Prime Meridian 147
Prosperina (goddess)
    274
Prussia, King of 184–5
Punch and Judy 29–30
purple laver 78–9
purse sein nets 40

Queen Anne's Revenge
    (ship) 174, 175
Quested, Cephas 187

Raffald, Elizabeth 78
Raleigh, Sir Walter 70,
    196
Ramsey Island 123
Ramsgate lifeboat 278
real de a ocho, see 'pieces
    of eight'
recipes/menus 69–70,
    74–8
Redoubtable (ship) 200
Reformation 251
Reis, Oruç 161
*Relation of the Great
    Sufferings and Strange
    Adventures of Henry*

Pitman, Chirugeon to the Late Duke of Monmouth, A (Pitman) 151
Remembrance Day 150
Richard II (Shakespeare) 11
Rime of the Ancient Mariner, The (Coleridge) 274
Robert, Earl of Gloucester 121
Robinson Crusoe (Defoe) 150–1
rock, stick of 67–8
Rodney, HMS 253
Romans 11, 82, 155–6, 250
ropes 40, 209, 219, 220, 223–5, 237–40, 248, 249, 254
Royal Air Force (RAF) 192, 204, 210
Royal Flying Corps 192
Royal James (ship) 195
Royal Marine Commandos 192
Royal Naval Air Service (RNAS) 192
Royal Navy 11, 12, 120, 142, 149, 161, 164, 175, 191–204, 208, 210–12, 223–6, 239, 244, 246, 248, 253–4, 280
Royal Pavilion, Brighton 16
Royal Society 148
'Rule Britannia!' 155
Russell, Dr Richard 15
Rutupiae 155
Ryde Pier 21

St Catherine 260

St Michael 260–1
St Paul's Cathedral 200
St Peter 79
St Senara church 263
salt-marsh plants 91–3
saltwater 34–5, 81, 91
sand, buried in 61–2
sand drawing/writing 64
sand sculptures 64
sandcastles 57, 62–3, 64
sand-dune plants 92, 93
Santa Cruz de Tenerife, Battle of 199
saucy postcards 23–4
Saxons 120
Scott, Sir Walter 277
scurvy 212–13
sea areas, by name 227, 228–36
sea greens 79–80
sea measurements 219–20
sea potatoes 101
sea salt 34–5, 81, 91
sea shanties, types of 246–7
sea urchins 101
seafood 40, 72–5, 79–83, 97
seashells 64, 87–91, 95–6, 100
seaside picnics 68–70
seawater 34–5, 81, 91
seaweed 64, 78–9, 100, 102, 104–7
Second World War 19, 20, 21, 28, 71, 132, 149, 150, 164–5, 196, 203, 227, 246
selkiefolk 264–5
Selkirk, Alexander 150–1
Senlac Hill 159

Shakespeare, William 11, 80, 271
shark eggs 102
shellfish 74–5, 80–3
shingle beaches 37–8, 120
Shipping Forecast (BBC) 226–36
'Ship Swallower' 123
ships' bells 220–2
ships, naming of 193–7, 250–1
Shovell, Sir Cloudesley 147
shrimps 74–5, 82
Simon, Able Seacat 244–6
Slade, Thomas 194
Sluys, Battle of 191
smugglers, see pirates
'Smuggler's Song, A' (Kipling) 178–9
Socialist Camp 19
Solent, Battle of the 194
Southend Pier 21
Southport Pier 21
Spanish Armada 143, 163–4, 196, 261
Speedwell (ship) 144
Spurn Head 132
Stamford Bridge, Battle of 159
Stevenson, Robert Louis 175
Stoychev, Petar 136
Suckling, Catherine 198
Suckling, Capt. Matthew 198
Suffolk, HMS 213
superstitions 271, 273–9
surfing/surfboarding 43, 44
swimming clubs 41–2

swimming pools 19, 42
swimwear 24–6, 27, 41

Tale of Two Cities, A
   (Dickens) 71
'Tam O'Shanter'
   (Burns) 253
Tasman Sea 145
Teach, Edward 174
'Teach's lights' 175
Tempest, The
   (Shakespeare) 271
1066 158–60
Thatch, Edward 174
Thulean Plateau 259
tides 33–4, 42, 100, 120
Tilbury docks 164
Time 246
Times 227
'toiling classes' 28
Tower of London 209
Trafalgar, Battle of 195,
   254
travellers' guides 25
Treasure Island
   (Stevenson) 175
Treatise of the Scurvy
   (Lind) 212

Trewella, Matthew 263
Trinity House 125, 191
Truro 73
Turner, Robert 80

United Kingdom Sailing
   Academy (UKSA)
   146

'Valiant Sailors, The'
   (Parker) 109
Vernon, Admiral 254
Victory, HMS 194–5,
   196, 200, 254
Vikings 11, 156–8
Violet SS 278

Wagner, Richard 277
Ward, Rev. Philip 201
Warrior, HMS 253
waterskiing 44
'Weather Shipping' 227
Webb, Capt. Matthew
   136
West Hoe Pier 146
whelk eggs 102
whelks 82, 83
whet 78

Whit Monday 17
White Cliffs of Dover
   132
'wild swimming' 42–3
William, Duke of
   Normandy 158–60
William I 120
Wimbledon, Lord 196
Wind in the Willows, The
   (Grahame) 55
windsurfing 44
winkles 82, 83
Wolsey, Cardinal 201
Women's Royal Naval
   Service (WRNS), *see*
   Wrens
World Heritage Sites
   131
wreckers *see* pirates
Wrens 192, 202–4

xebecs 161

Yangtze River 245
Yorkston, James 65

Zennor, Mermaid of
   263

To sea, to sea! The calm is o'er;
The wanton water leaps in sport,
And rattles down the pebbly shore;
The dolphin wheels, the sea-cows snort,
And unseen Mermaids' pearly song
Comes bubbling up, the weeds among.
Fling broad the sail, dip deep the oar:
To sea, to sea! The calm is o'er.

To sea, to sea! Our wide-winged bark
Shall billowy cleave its sunny way,
And with its shadow, fleet and dark,
Break the caved Tritons' azure day,
Like mighty eagle soaring light
O'er antelopes on Alpine height.
The anchor heaves, the ship swings free,
The sails swell full. To sea, to sea!

THOMAS LOVELL BEDDOES